For Steve W.

Yahoo! Chat Clients

This book contains compiler BASIC (PowerBASIC) and C++ (Borland C++ Builder) source code of a Yahoo! Chat client. Yahoo! Chat was a public chat room service created in 1997. It was closed down in 2019 and remains closed as of 2024. I was one of the first two people to reverse engineer the Yahoo! Chat protocol. I decided to create a chat client but was, at the time, unaware of the Windows API (Application Programming Interface) or how to access the internet on a computer (TCP/IP or Transmission Control Protocol / Internet Protocol via the WSOCK32 DLL or dynamic link library) or the inner workings of a chat client. I did, however, know C, C++, compiler BASIC, and x86 assembly. I created a packet sniffer that allowed me to compare what I typed in chat (using another name, using Yahoo's own chat client, in the same room) to what the server sent to my client. This is most of how you reverse engineer a chat client. My client includes two Sysop codes that no other programmer, to my knowledge, is aware of yet. I learned about programming in Windows using a book by Charles Petzold called Programming Windows. It is highly recommended for low level Windows coding.

I reverse engineered the Yahoo! Chat protocol while spending my time in the Programming:1 and Programming:2 rooms on Yahoo! Chat. There were four notable persons there. First, there was David, also known as Master Deep, who ended up creating the popular Yahelite chat client. I am mentioned in his client as helping with some chat technicalities: under the name io_0x45. Second, there was a person who I mentored who created the first yahoo chat client for Visual Basic. This opened up chat coding to many other programmers. Third, there was an employee of Yahoo (screen name 127_0_0_1 or local host) who helped us navigate some of the login procedures of the Yahoo chat system. David and I competed in creating the smallest chat client. I had the x86 assembly Windows client and he created a small, text based client in C.

I created chat clients using x86 assembly language, compiler BASIC, C, and C++. The specific language software used were as follows: 32-bit Microsoft Macro Assembler (MASM32), the 32-bit PowerBASIC compiler for Windows [the core language was created using over 400,000 lines of hand coded assembly by a single programmer… Robert "Bob" Zale], Microsoft Visual C++ but used as a C compiler (utilizing no C++), and Borland's C++ Builder which used the OWL (Object Windows Library) and VCL (Visual Component Library) that allowed for fast creation of the Windows graphical user interface (GUI). Each software package had its pros and cons. There is often a big difference between a programming language and the actual implementations of that programming language. Languages, by themselves, are perfect but the actual products (compilers and IDEs [Integrated Development Environment]) are not.

MASM32 is an excellent assembler and is freely available via Microsoft. This is not the unstructured assembly code of the past. MASM32 has IF, WHILE, and UNTIL statements and can INVOKE (call) functions. MASM32's macros allow a programmer to basically define their own language. The best thing about assembly programming is that you can code and code and code and the executable hardly grows in size. The chat client source code file was 62k bytes long: while its executable was only 17k bytes. In high level languages it is easy to add a single line that turns your code into bloatware, especially in the C++ implementation I used. The chat client executable in MASM32 is smaller than a compressed JPEG picture of the actual client running. This client was a prototype but was advanced enough to use a color Rich Edit control. This client will be described in detail.

PowerBASIC for Windows (32-bit) is my favorite windows compiler and at one time I had used every compiler I could get my hands on. I like PowerBASIC's 16-bit DOS compiler even more. The beauty of PowerBASIC is that it is a simple compiler, language, and IDE. Microsoft's Visual C++ is a better compiler as far as compactness or speed of code generated. However, PowerBASIC is close (in speed and size) while allowing for a simple language (BASIC) to be utilized. This is not the spaghetti code BASIC of the past. PowerBASIC supports pointers (great for interfacing with C or C++ code), six signed / unsigned integers, five floating point types, four string types, subroutines, functions, memory management, user defined TYPES, 80-bit floating point variables, and built-in ARRAY manipulation keywords. PowerBASIC also includes a built-in x86 assembler and emits machine-code standalone executables. Programming is structured with no line numbers necessary, IF / THEN / ELSE, SELECT / CASE, EXIT / ITERATE, FOR / NEXT, WHILE / WEND, and DO / LOOP control structures and many useful and advanced string functions. The BASIC chat client executable was about 45k bytes in size. PowerBASIC is like a miniature (written in assembler) C compiler with BASIC syntax. PowerBASIC and MASM32 needed only one source file; whereas Visual C and C++ Builder needed several files. All of Windows' graphical elements could be encapsulated in the PowerBASIC source code file. The PowerBASIC IDE (integrated development environment) is very lightweight, compiler speed is excellent, and there are virtually no bugs. There is also an integrated debugger. Even compiler switches can be manipulated in the source code file.

The C client was created using Microsoft's Visual C++ compiler. The compiler itself is great as far as code generation, as long as you are familiar with and select the proper compiler options. By adding nop or no-operation assembly codes (0x90) to the source file, you can search for them later and examine the actual machine code being created by the compiler. You can learn a lot of tricks for MASM32 when examining the emitted code of Visual C++'s compiler. The client executable was about 30k bytes in size. The Visual C++ IDE is huge and always felt like it was taking over the entire machine. The documentation was extensive. Compared to BASIC, what is annoying with C are all the necessary brackets and semicolons. Also C's null terminated strings and pointers often end up security problems. BASIC is slightly slower with the string functions but they never can over-run the destination string. Pointers can also be avoided and are mostly used in PowerBASIC to interface with C code. C is a great language but it is also unsafe. Even the best programmers can make mistakes that can be exploited later. That said, one of my favorite books is: The C Programming Language by Brian W. Kernigham and Dennis M. Ritchie.

The C++ Yahoo! Chat client was created using Borland's C++ Builder. This client was the most visually stunning because of the OWL and VCL libraries. C++ is a decent language but its implementations are often not good as far as executable size. C++ Builder's compiler emitted bloatware. The C++ client's executable ended up being 813k bytes or 18+ times larger than the BASIC and C clients. It was, however, easy to build the visual interface and use advanced visual elements. Borland's IDE made it feel like you were lucky that the code even compiled. The compile times were slow compared to the BASIC and C compilers. C++ Builder created large and slow executable files.

Now would be a great time for someone to resurrect a chat client like Yahoo! Chat. There were millions of people on the system and it was a great social experiment. For years it was the wild West of the internet. I am dedicating this book to the fourth notable person in chat: my friend, Steve, who passed away at 43. I met Steve on Yahoo! Chat, in the programming rooms, and we continued e-mailing ideas about computers and electronics until 2021. We would often start up Nine Inch Nails or Led Zeppelin CD's at the same time so that we could listen together as we typed in chat… while I was busy creating the Yahoo! Chat clients that are present in this book.

In the paragraphs ahead, the assembly language client program will be extensively described. The C and assembly clients were very similar in structure and were not included in the book. The C client was easier to follow but contained several files due to the Visual C++ implementation of the C language for Windows. The assembly client description shows what is needed for a chat client at the bare metal level (using C or assembly). The included DLLs were as follows: WINDOWS, USER32 [the graphical user interface], KERNEL32 [the operating system loaded into protected memory], WSOCK32 [sockets or the internet code], MASM32, GDI32 [the graphics device interface], and SHELL32. I created my own string routines for the assembly language version of the chat client.

In the assembly client, two compiler directives are given. The first being ".386" for 80386 code generation. The second being ".model flat, stdcall" for a flat memory model and using the Win32 calling convention for functions. The source file is split into data (.data) and code (.code) sections. In the data section there are "db" or data bytes (8-bits) and "dd" or data double word (4 bytes long or 32-bits, for example the colors used on screen). Also .data? is used to denote variables (using question marks). The code section contains the keyword "start:" which invokes GetModuleHandle, LoadLibrary (for the rich edit control's DLL or RICHED32.DLL), and invokes WinMain. After WinMain ends (at program termination) it calls FreeLibrary and ExitProcess. WinMain is a function that is the Windows application entry point.

Chat clients are mostly about string manipulation and net input and output. String macros (ex. $strLen) include: New, Del (delete), Zero (for nulling the string), Mov (move), Cat and Two and Four (for concatenation), and memCopy. Advanced string macros include: Trim (delete spaces from each end), Len (length), Pos (the position of one string within another string), Char (the character at a certain position), Mid (for adding a string at a position) and Comp (to compare two strings). List macros include: Add, Del (delete), and Chk (check or find if a name is in a list). The Stripper function cuts out elements such as HTML codes.

Other macros are included for messaging: $Box (show a message box), $Status (change the status bar message), $Tell (show in the rich edit box or the main screen output), $SendRich (send the rich edit control a message), $YCHT (send the outgoing packet, which starts with "YCHT"). Later chat clients sent a packet starting with "YMSG" and had MD5 encryption.

Windows functions include: WinMain, lstWndProc, and TopXY (center the window). The function lstWndProc was introduced using SetWindowLong. Internet related functions include: CreateSocket, InitSocket, Delay (which allows waiting for a net response), YCHT_IN (where incoming yahoo chat packets are decoded) and Parse (cutting up the packet using a specific parse string). YCHT_IN utilizes a 65536 byte input buffer. Codes that are recognized include: Login, Logout, FF, Sysop.1, Sysop.2, Advertise, Error, Roll Dice, Mail, Message, Packet 71, Help, Away, Graffiti, Invite, Leave, Not Online, New Room, Roommates, Message buddy, Speak, Think, and Emote.

Included Easter egg functions use the InOral procedure or checking for a word or phrase that was said by someone. Mischief fixers include Retro or retroactive ignore where all the past messages from a person on ignore are erased. I was the first to have this functionality as it helped deal with spammers. Also helping was Repeats where the person repeating text automatically goes on retroactive ignore. And Filter where the client would not show: blank lines, ignored people, long lines, shouters, repeaters, etcetera. Other functions include Form and Form2 (string concatenation), CleanAll (clears the screen and status bar), and Resolve (dealing with finding strings within strings).

The address 10.0.0.1 was the proxy IP address [proxies act as an intermediary between your computer and the internet]. The cookie server was located at edit.yahoo.com. A username and password are passed using an HTTP "GET" command [GET /config/ncclogin] to obtain a cookie. The cookie is good for about a month and must be stripped out of the response. The cookie must be used to log on to the internet location cs.chat.yahoo.com or the yahoo chat server. These addresses and ports were obtained by an ASCII scan of the official Yahoo! Chat client. I wrote a C program to extract all relevant ASCII codes. The client parser cuts packets with the following header: "YCHT",1,1,1,1,0 that can show up multiple times in packets. There was a 10 minute Windows timer that would be used to send a "stay alive" packet or "YCHT",0,0,1,0,0,0,0,98,0,0,0,0 to the server. This was tricky to figure out initially. The original clients kept getting dropped by Yahoo.

The assembly client responded to text commands that started with a forward slash or /. Where /c utilized the username and password to obtain a cookie (this was slow). And /l logged into the chat server using the most recent cookie (this was fast). And /r changed to a new chat room, often Programming:2 for me. And /q quit would log out of the server. And /x toggles the use of the proxy address. And /e sent an emote, /t sent a thought bubble, and /a sent an away message. There were three, alterable, lists: /b or buddy, /n or normal, and /i or ignore. The buddy and ignore lists were shown with /z command or show lists. And /o cleared the entire screen. And /k "killed" or ignored the person and retroactively erased all their posts. And /v was used to invite people to the room. And /j allowed you to join a PM or private messaging, while /p allowed the PM to be sent. And /w warned the person PMing (who was not a buddy)... their text would show up only in the status window (to prevent PM spamming). And /m toggled alert mode on and off. And /f showed the profile of a person (these were found at the internet location http://profiles.yahoo.com), while /u showed the most recently sent chat URL [Uniform Resource

Locator, invoking the ShellExecute function], and /y copied text from the screen. And /! invoked a secure mode where only packets from people on your friends list were shown. When the room was under heavy attack this would allow dumping all packets by just reading who they were from. This made the client unbootable. Everything in this paragraph was shown on screen by typing /h or /? or accessing the rudimentary help system. And /d was the debug mode where the actual packets were shown along with how they were translated.

This paragraph relays the "About" information for the assembly language client. The client was called Mercer beta 1. The name was after Trent Reznor's hometown of Mercer, Pennsylvania. The client was created with the 32 bit MASM32 assembler and the WIN32 API. The packets were sniffed to reverse engineer the client. The assembly client had built in colors for your friends. Others chatters were shown in gray.

The code section INVOKES WinMain followed by LoadIcon, LoadCursor, and RegisterClassEx [used prior to CreateWindowEx]. Then the code invokes GetSystemMetrics [this retrieves values in pixels] and TopXY. Following that were invocations of CreateWindowEx, ShowWindow, and UpdateWindow. Sockets or the windows internet interface was started by invoking WSAStartup [this function initiates use of the WinSock DLL]. There is a message pump loop utilizing GetMessage, TranslateMessage, and DispatchMessage.

The WndProc callback function contains the message pump. Hooks are used: they are a mechanism by which the client intercepts events. Below "WM_" stands for Windows message. Some windows messages hooked are WM_CREATE (invokes multiple CreateWindowEx graphical control elements and initializes the program variables), WM_DESTROY (invokes closesocket and WSACleanup) and WM_SIZE (invokes MoveWindow that changes the position and dimensions of a window). Under WM_SOCKET there is FD_CONNECT [connection is completed]. The cookie uses port 1123 with the proxy and port 80 without the proxy. Chat uses port 8002 and invokes "send" [transmission of a message from a socket to its peer]. FD_READ [read internet data] invokes ioctlsocket [a function that sets the input or output mode of a socket], and "recv" [a function that receives data from a socket and stores it in a buffer]. There is FD_CLOSE [connection is closed] that invokes closesocket. Another message is WM_TIMER [a Windows low priority timer] for the stay alive packet. In the procedure called YCHT a function is invoked called "send" [sends socket data that is stored in a buffer] to output packets to the server. Its output buffer is 2084 bytes long.

The procedure called lstWndProc resolves and translates all of the keyboard commands. The commands start with a forward slash as

8

stated in a paragraph above. The procedure invokes CallWindowProc [this function passes message information to a window procedure]. Another procedure called InitSocket uses (invokes) several functions including socket [the function creates a new socket descriptor], WSAAsyncSelect [the function requests Windows message notifications of socket events: connect, read, and close], htons [host byte order translated into network byte order], inet_addr [the function turns a string to an integer used as an internet address], gethostbyname, connect, and closesocket. Other rich edit box related (sent) messages include WM_SETFONT, WM_GETTEXTLENGTH, WM_COPY, and WM_SETTEXT (also used for setting the status box text). There are three places to send messages: ID_TEXT (the user typed client commands and text being sent to others), ID_RICH (the main chat text window with the multiple-person conversation), and ID_STAT (the status line text).

Compiler BASIC and C++ language Yahoo! Chat clients are included in this book. The BASIC version is shown first because it is easy to understand and not as long as the C++ source code. Only two includes are needed: WIN32API (the Windows 32-bit operating system) and WSOCK32 (windows sockets or the code used to read and write to the internet). If color text was needed then RICHEDIT was also needed: to program the rich edit control. Many, other, versions of the BASIC client had RICHEDIT (color text). The C++ version is shown second. The C version is, unfortunately, missing. The assembly version was described in detail above.

The actual source code follows for the PowerBASIC and Borland C++ Builder versions of a chat client. Both are compilers and both are RAD [Rapid Applications Development] languages, moreso with the C++ Builder program. The C++ client is officially called "PeaceChat"; while the BASIC client is called "uChatx86" (code name "NEW DEAL 06"). Both clients were memory safe, compared to the assembly and C version.

The Borland C++ Builder client executable was 813k bytes in size. The PowerBASIC client executable was 45k bytes in size. The actual C++ code takes up 95k bytes. The actual BASIC code takes up 20k bytes. What is not shown are the 29k bytes of header files and 193k bytes of DFM (that describe the forms) files for the C++ client. The C++ client included two picture files (6k bytes and 14k bytes) and an icon file (1k bytes). Comparison of the C++ and BASIC files is like comparing apples to oranges. But this is the real world where there is an efficient BASIC compiler with easy Windows and internet access. And a very complex C++ compiler using OWL and VCL. The C++ client code was spread over 15 files and had a total of 2,975 lines of code. The BASIC client code was contained in one file and had a total of 681 lines of code. Clients as small as ~300 lines of code, with reduced features, were created in PowerBASIC.

Photo on back cover, upper: MASM32 client

Photo on back cover, lower: PowerBASIC client

YAHOO CHAT CLIENT 1

uChatx86

PowerBASIC Windows compiler

Dr. Phillip M. Angelos

45 kilobyte executable

```
'
' Dr. Phillip M. Angelos
' Yahoo chat client
' PowerBASIC compiler
'

' Compiler directives
#COMPILE EXE
#DEBUG ERROR OFF
#DIM ALL
#OPTION VERSION4
#REGISTER NONE
#INCLUDE "WIN32API.INC"
#INCLUDE "WSOCK32.INC"

' Equates
%ID_TEXT     = 116
%ID_RECIEVE  = 118
%ID_RICH     = 200
%ID_TIMER    = 218
%ID_COOKIE   = 236
%ID_STAT     = 250

' Global variables
GLOBAL hDlg AS LONG
GLOBAL theplace AS STRING
GLOBAL theroomin AS STRING
GLOBAL UserName AS STRING
GLOBAL savePass AS STRING
GLOBAL saveUser AS STRING
GLOBAL theuser AS STRING
GLOBAL theignored AS STRING
GLOBAL theloginstate AS LONG
GLOBAL gSpammer AS STRING
GLOBAL gSpamCnt AS LONG
GLOBAL gLastSaid AS STRING
GLOBAL thetcp AS STRING
GLOBAL theroomies AS STRING
GLOBAL gdebug AS LONG
GLOBAL gproxy AS LONG
GLOBAL gPM AS STRING
GLOBAL rest AS STRING
' added
GLOBAL gRoomList AS STRING
GLOBAL gResolve AS STRING
GLOBAL gWarning AS STRING
GLOBAL gAlert AS STRING
```

```
GLOBAL gURL AS STRING
GLOBAL gURLChars AS STRING
GLOBAL gCookie AS STRING

' Name Resolution
SUB Resolve
   IF rest = "" THEN EXIT SUB
   LOCAL isat AS LONG
   LOCAL temp AS STRING
   isat = INSTR(gResolve, "[" + rest)
   IF isat <> 0 THEN
        temp = MID$(gResolve,isat+1)
        rest = EXTRACT$(temp,"]")
   'ELSE
      'OutStatus "UNRESOLVEABLE"
   END IF
END SUB


' Add Resolution
SUB ResAdd(BYVAL dude AS STRING)
    IF INSTR(gResolve, "[" + dude + "]") = 0 THEN gResolve = gResolve
+ "[" + dude + "]"
END SUB


' Status message
SUB OutStatus(BYVAL sMessage AS STRING)
  CONTROL SET TEXT hDlg, %ID_STAT, sMessage
END SUB

' Login
SUB TheLogin
  LOCAL thepass AS STRING

  IF LEN(UserName) > 0 AND PARSECOUNT(UserName," ") = 3 THEN
    UserName = TRIM$(UserName)
    theuser  = TRIM$(PARSE$(UserName, " ",2))
    saveUser = theuser
    thepass  = TRIM$(PARSE$(UserName, " ",3))
    savePass = thepass
  ELSE
    theuser  = saveUser
    thepass  = savePass
  END IF

  IF (theuser = "") OR (thepass = "") THEN
    theloginstate = 0
```

13

```
      OutStatus "INVALID_USER_PASS"
      EXIT SUB
   END IF

   theloginstate = 2 ' aka during

   ' Ask For Cookie
   LOCAL iport AS LONG
   LOCAL iaddy AS STRING
   IF gproxy = 1 THEN
      iport = 1123
      iaddy = "10.0.0.1"
   ELSE
      iport = 80
      iaddy = "edit.yahoo.com"
   END IF

   TCP OPEN PORT iport AT iaddy AS #2
   TCP NOTIFY #2, RECV TO hDlg AS %ID_COOKIE
   SLEEP 250
   TCP PRINT #2, "GET /config/login?.src=&login=" + theuser +
"&passwd=" + thepass + "&n=1 HTTP/1.0" + CHR$(13,10) + "Accept: */*"
& CHR$(13,10) + "Accept: text/html" + CHR$(13,10,13,10)
   TCP PRINT #2, ""

END SUB

' Output to Screen
SUB Tell(BYVAL theoutput AS STRING)
   LOCAL outptext AS STRING
   CONTROL GET TEXT hDlg, %ID_RICH TO outptext
   'blow out buffer
   outptext = LEFT$(outptext, 16000)
   CONTROL SET TEXT hDlg, %ID_RICH, theoutput + $CRLF + outptext
END SUB

' Clear Text
SUB Clean
   CONTROL SET TEXT hDlg, %ID_TEXT, ""
   CONTROL SET FOCUS hDlg, %ID_TEXT
END SUB

' TCP (net) Output
SUB YCHT(BYVAL thecom AS LONG, BYVAL thedata AS STRING)
   TCP SEND #1, "YCHT" & CHR$(0,0,1,0,0,0,0) & CHR$(thecom) &
CHR$(0,0) & _
```

```
                    CHR$(INT(LEN(thedata)/256)) & CHR$(LEN(thedata) MOD
256) & thedata
END SUB

' Dialog Callback
CALLBACK FUNCTION DlgCall

' Stay-Alive Timer
IF CBMSG = %WM_TIMER AND CBWPARAM = %ID_TIMER THEN
  IF theloginstate = 1 THEN TCP SEND #1, "YCHT" &
CHR$(0,0,1,0,0,0,0,98,0,0,0,0)
END IF

' Sizing Window
IF CBMSG = %WM_SIZE THEN
  LOCAL scrx&, scry&
  DIALOG PIXELS hDlg, LOWRD(CBLPARAM), HIWRD(CBLPARAM) TO UNITS
scrx&, scry&
  CONTROL SET SIZE hDlg, %ID_STAT, scrx& - 4, 13 '- 101
  CONTROL SET SIZE hDlg, %ID_TEXT, scrx& - 4, 13 '- 101
  CONTROL SET SIZE hDlg, %ID_RICH, scrx& - 4, scry& - 35
END IF

' Closing routines
IF CBMSG = %WM_CLOSE THEN
  TCP CLOSE #1
  TCP CLOSE #2
  KillTimer CBHNDL, %ID_TIMER
END IF

' Startup Code
IF CBMSG = %WM_INITDIALOG THEN
  'vars
  theloginstate = 0
  theroomin = "Programming:1"
  gdebug = 0
  gproxy = 0
  gWarning = "Error: Undelivered"

  'URL valid characters
  LOCAL uch AS LONG
  FOR uch = 33 TO 126
    gURLChars = gURLChars + CHR$(uch)
  NEXT

END IF
```

```
' Cookie Retrieval Code
IF CBMSG = %ID_COOKIE THEN
 SELECT CASE LOWRD(CBLPARAM)

  'Internet Read
  CASE %FD_READ
   LOCAL buffer AS STRING
   LOCAL tcpcook AS STRING
   tcpcook = ""
   buffer = SPACE$(4000)
   DO
     TCP RECV #2, 4000, buffer
     tcpcook = tcpcook + buffer
   LOOP WHILE LEN(buffer)
   TCP CLOSE #2
   theloginstate = 3

   STATIC thecookie AS STRING
   STATIC nthecookie AS STRING
   LOCAL thecs AS LONG
   LOCAL thece AS LONG
   thecs = INSTR(tcpcook, "Y=v=")
   tcpcook = MID$(tcpcook,thecs,500)
   thece = INSTR(tcpcook, ";")
   thecookie = MID$(tcpcook, 1, thece)

   thecs = INSTR(tcpcook, "T=z=")
   tcpcook = MID$(tcpcook,thecs,500)
   thece = INSTR(tcpcook, ";") -1
   nthecookie = MID$(tcpcook, 1, thece)

   thecookie = thecookie + " " + nthecookie

   IF LEN(thecookie) > 20 THEN
      gCookie = thecookie
      OutStatus "COOKIE_VALID"
   ELSE
      OutStatus "COOKIE_FAILURE"
   END IF

  '...
 END SELECT
END IF

' Recieve TCP
```

```
IF CBMSG = %ID_RECIEVE THEN

  LOCAL tcpraw AS STRING
  tcpraw = SPACE$(4000)
  TCP RECV #1, 4000, tcpraw

  LOCAL chzero AS LONG
  FOR chzero = 1 TO LEN(tcpraw)
    IF ASC(MID$(tcpraw,chzero,1)) = 0 THEN MID$(tcpraw,chzero,1) =
CHR$(1)
  NEXT chzero

' Slicer (parsing)
  LOCAL theslice AS LONG
  LOCAL thetcpx AS STRING
  chzero = PARSECOUNT(tcpraw, "YCHT" & CHR$(1,1,1,1))
  FOR theslice = 1 TO chzero - 1
    thetcpx = "YCHT" + CHR$(1,1,1,1) + PARSE$(tcpraw,"YCHT" &
CHR$(1,1,1,1),theslice + 1)

' Debug Mode
    IF gdebug = 1 THEN
        CALL Tell(thetcpx)
    END IF

' Slice Processing
    thetcp = thetcpx

    LOCAL thecommand AS STRING
    LOCAL theerror AS STRING
    thecommand = HEX$(ASC(thetcp,12),2)
    theerror   = HEX$(ASC(thetcp,13),2) + HEX$(ASC(thetcp,14),2)

    IF MID$(thetcp,1,11) <> "YCHT" & CHR$(1,1,1,1,1,1,1) THEN CALL
Tell("[ERROR:HEADER]")
    IF (theerror <> "0101") THEN
      CALL Tell ("[ERROR:" + thecommand + "]")
      EXIT FUNCTION
    END IF
    thetcp = MID$(thetcp,17)
    LOCAL themark AS STRING
    LOCAL theperson AS STRING
    theperson = PARSE$(thetcp, CHR$(192,128), 2)
    LOCAL thewholeperson AS STRING
    thewholeperson = TRIM$(theperson)
```

```
'  Command
    SELECT CASE thecommand
      CASE "01"
        theloginstate = 1
        OutStatus "LOGIN"
        CALL Clean
        'enter room
        CALL YCHT(17, theroomin)
      CASE "02"
        OutStatus "LOGOUT"
        CALL Clean
        'continue...
        theloginstate = 0
        TCP CLOSE #1
      CASE "41" 'Speech
        themark = ":"
      CASE "42" 'Think
        themark = "?"
      CASE "43" 'Emotion
        themark = "*"
      CASE "45" 'PMing
        theperson = PARSE$(thetcp, CHR$(192,128), 1)
        IF INSTR(gRoomList, "[" + theperson + "]") = 0 OR _
           INSTR(theignored, "[" + theperson + "]") <> 0 THEN
                OutStatus "EXTERNAL_PM: " + theperson
                IF (gWarning <> "" ) THEN
                    CALL YCHT(69, theuser & CHR$(1) & theperson &
CHR$(1) & gWarning)
                END IF
        ELSE
            themark = "==>"
        END IF
      CASE "21" 'Away
        LOCAL awaymsg AS STRING
        LOCAL awaynum AS LONG
        theperson = PARSE$(thetcp, CHR$(192,128), 1)
        awaynum = VAL(PARSE$(thetcp, CHR$(192,128), 3)) + 1
        IF awaynum = 11 THEN
          awaymsg = PARSE$(thetcp, CHR$(192,128), 4)
        ELSE
          awaymsg = "" 'PARSE$(awaymsg, ",", awaynum)
        END IF
        IF awaynum = 1 THEN
          OutStatus "BACK: " + theperson
        ELSE
          OutStatus "AWAY: " + theperson + " " + awaymsg
```

```
        END IF
      CASE "17" 'Invite parse 2+3
        OutStatus "INVITE: " + theperson + " TO: " + PARSE$(thetcp,
CHR$(198,128), 2)
      CASE "11" 'Enter
        LOCAL rmlist AS STRING
        rmlist = PARSE$(thetcp,CHR$(192,128),5)
        IF INSTR(rmlist,theuser) <> 0 THEN
          theroomin = PARSE$(thetcp,CHR$(192,128),1)
          theplace = theroomin

          'new stuff
          CALL Clean

        ' get roommates
        LOCAL zero AS LONG
        zero = INSTR(rmlist,"#")
        WHILE (zero >= 1 AND MID$(rmlist,zero+10,1) = "#")
            rmlist = MID$(rmlist,1,zero-1) + ", " + MID$
(rmlist,zero+11)
            zero = INSTR(rmlist,"#")
        WEND
        zero = INSTR(rmlist,"#")
        IF (zero >=1 AND MID$(rmlist,zero+8,1) = "#") THEN
            rmlist = MID$(rmlist,1,zero-1)
        END IF
          CALL Tell($CRLF + "ROOMMATES: [" + rmlist + "]" + $CRLF)
          OutStatus "ROOM: " + theplace
          gRoomList = "[" + rmlist + "]"
          REPLACE ", " WITH "][" IN gRoomList
          zero = PARSECOUNT(rmlist, ", ")
          LOCAL dummy AS LONG
          FOR dummy = 1 TO zero
              CALL ResAdd(PARSE$(rmlist, ", ", dummy))
          NEXT

          'continue...
        ELSE
          theperson = EXTRACT$(rmlist,CHR$(2))
          gRoomList = gRoomList + "[" + theperson + "]"
          CALL ResAdd(theperson)
          OutStatus "ENTER: " + theperson
        END IF
      CASE "12" 'Leave
        LOCAL lbFindat AS LONG
        REPLACE "[" + theperson + "]" WITH "" IN gRoomList
```

```basic
        OutStatus "LEAVE: " + theperson
    CASE ELSE
        OutStatus "[CODE:" + thecommand + "]"
    END SELECT

    ' Speak-Think-Emote
    IF LEN(themark) > 0 AND INSTR(theignored, "[" + thewholeperson +
"]") = 0 THEN

        LOCAL theoral AS STRING
        theoral = PARSE$(thetcp, CHR$(192,128), 3)
        theperson = LEFT$(theperson + SPACE$(16),16) + " " + themark
+ " "

        'alert
        IF gAlert <> "" AND INSTR(theoral,gAlert) <> 0 THEN
            MSGBOX "Alert: " + gAlert
        END IF

        'continue...
        LOCAL theyest AS STRING
        LOCAL thecont AS LONG
        LOCAL clrcut AS LONG
        thecont = PARSECOUNT(theoral, CHR$(27))
        FOR clrcut = 1 TO thecont
            theyest = REMAIN$(theoral, CHR$(27))
            theyest = EXTRACT$(theyest, "m")
            REPLACE CHR$(27) + theyest + "m" WITH "" IN theoral
        NEXT clrcut

        thecont = PARSECOUNT(theoral, "<")
        FOR clrcut = 1 TO thecont
            theyest = REMAIN$(theoral, "<")
            theyest = EXTRACT$(theyest, ">")
            REPLACE "<" + theyest + ">" WITH "" IN theoral
        NEXT clrcut

        ' URL testing

        LOCAL urlstart AS LONG
        urlstart = INSTR(LCASE$(theoral),"www.")
        IF urlstart = 0 THEN urlstart = INSTR(LCASE$
(theoral),"http://")
        IF urlstart <> 0 THEN
            LOCAL urlend AS LONG
            urlend = VERIFY(urlstart,theoral, gURLChars)
```

```
            gURL = MID$(theoral,urlstart,urlend-urlstart)
            OutStatus "URL: " + gURL
        END IF


        'Filtration Subsystem
        LOCAL willshow AS LONG
        willshow = 1
        LOCAL ioral AS STRING
        ioral = UCASE$(ioral)
        ' tags
        IF INSTR(theoral, "<URL=") <> 0 OR _
           INSTR(theoral, "<PM=")  <> 0 OR _
           INSTR(theoral, "<SND=") <> 0 THEN
               willshow = 0
               OutStatus "TAG_USED: " + theperson
        END IF
        ' macros
        IF PARSECOUNT(theoral,CHR$(13)) >= 2 OR _
           PARSECOUNT(theoral,CHR$(10)) >= 2 THEN
           willshow = 0
           OutStatus "MACRO_USED: " + theperson
        END IF
        ' long line
        IF LEN(theoral) > 300 THEN
            willshow = 0
            OutStatus "LONGLINE: " + theperson
        END IF
        ' shouter neutralized
        IF theoral = ioral THEN theoral = "(s) " + LCASE$(theoral)
        ' repeats
        IF gLastSaid = (theperson + theoral) THEN
            willshow = 0
            OutStatus "REPEATER: " + theperson
        END IF


        ' finally output it
        IF willshow = 1 AND TRIM$(theoral) <> "" THEN
            CALL Tell(theperson + theoral)
            gLastSaid = theperson + theoral
        END IF

    'continue...
    END IF
  NEXT theslice
END IF
```

```
' Process Menu
IF CBMSG = %WM_COMMAND THEN

' Typed Input
LOCAL usertyped AS STRING
CONTROL GET TEXT CBHNDL, %ID_TEXT TO usertyped

' Textbox RETURN key
  IF CBCTL = %ID_TEXT AND INSTR(usertyped, $CRLF) THEN
      REPLACE $CRLF WITH "" IN usertyped
      IF LEN(usertyped) = 0 THEN EXIT IF

    IF MID$(usertyped,1,1) = "/" THEN
        LOCAL rcom AS STRING
        rest = TRIM$(MID$(usertyped,4))
        rcom = MID$(usertyped,2,1)

        'room
        IF rcom = "r" THEN
            CALL YCHT(17, rest)
        END IF

        'close down = quit
        IF rcom = "q" THEN
            TCP CLOSE #1
            CONTROL SET TEXT hDlg, %ID_RICH, ""
            OutStatus "LOGGED_OUT"
        END IF

        'Cookie
        IF rcom = "l" THEN
            IF gCookie = "" THEN
                OutStatus "NOCOOKIE"
            ELSE
                TCP CLOSE #1
                SLEEP 250
                CONTROL SET TEXT hDlg, %ID_RICH, ""
                'proxy stuff
                  LOCAL xaddy AS STRING
                  IF gproxy = 1 THEN xaddy = "10.0.0.1" ELSE xaddy =
"jcs.chat.dcn.yahoo.com"

                  TCP OPEN PORT 8001 AT xaddy AS #1 TIMEOUT 0
                  TCP NOTIFY #1, RECV TO hDlg AS %ID_RECIEVE
                  SLEEP 250
                  'Login
```

```
                CALL YCHT(1,theuser & CHR$(1) + gCookie)

                CONTROL SET FOCUS hDlg, %ID_TEXT
            END IF
        END IF

        'Login
        IF rcom = "c" THEN
            UserName = usertyped
            usertyped = ""
                    TCP CLOSE #2
                    SLEEP 250
                    CALL TheLogin
                    theloginstate = 0
        END IF

        'away
        IF rcom = "a" THEN
            IF rest = "" THEN rest = "BRB"
            CALL YCHT(33, theuser & CHR$(192,128) & "10" &
CHR$(192,128) & rest)
        END IF

        'think
        IF rcom = "t" THEN
            CALL YCHT(67, theplace & CHR$(1,27,91,42) & "m" &
CHR$(27,91) & "36m" & _
                CHR$(27,91) & "x1m" & ". o 0 ( " + MID$(usertyped,4)
+ " )" )
        END IF

        'emote
        IF rcom = "e" THEN
            CALL YCHT(67, theplace & CHR$(1,27,91,42) & "m" &
CHR$(27,91) & "36m" & _
                CHR$(27,91) & "x1m" & MID$(usertyped,4))
        END IF

        'help
        IF rcom = "?" THEN
            CALL Tell($CRLF + "HELP: /c user pass, /l login, /r room,
/e emote, /t think, " +
            "/a away, /i ignore, /o clear, /d debug, /v invite, /g
GOTO, /x proxy, " + _
            "/m roomlist, /f profile, /w warning, /b bindPM, /p
PMing, " + _
```

```
                "/u alert, /n navigate, /q quit" + $CRLF)
END IF

'clear screen
IF rcom = "o" THEN
    OutStatus "Clear"
    CONTROL SET TEXT hDlg, %ID_RICH, ""
END IF

'proxy
IF rcom = "x" THEN
    IF gproxy = 0 THEN
        gproxy = 1
        OutStatus "PROXY"
    ELSE
        gproxy = 0
        OutStatus "NOPROXY"
    END IF
END IF

'debug
IF rcom = "d" THEN
    IF gdebug = 0 THEN
        gdebug = 1
        OutStatus "DEBUG"
    ELSE
        gdebug = 0
        OutStatus "NODEBUG"
    END IF
END IF

'invite
IF rcom = "v" THEN
    CALL Resolve
    IF rest = "" THEN EXIT IF
    CALL YCHT(23, rest)
    OutStatus "INVITED: " + rest
END IF

'goto
IF rcom = "g" THEN
    CALL Resolve
    IF rest = "" THEN EXIT IF
    CALL YCHT(37, rest)
    OutStatus "GOTO: " + rest
END IF
```

```
'bindPM
IF rcom = "b" THEN
    CALL Resolve
    gPM = rest
    IF gPM = "" THEN
        OutStatus "UNBOUND"
    ELSE
        OutStatus "BINDPM: " + rest
    END IF
END IF

'PMing
IF rcom = "p" THEN
    IF gPM = "" THEN
        OutStatus "NOTBOUND"
    ELSE
        IF rest = "" THEN EXIT IF
        CALL YCHT(69, theuser & CHR$(1) & gPM & CHR$(1) &
rest)
        CALL Tell(LEFT$(gPM + SPACE$(16),16) + " <== " +
rest)
    END IF
END IF

'Profile
IF rcom = "f" THEN
    CALL Resolve
    LOCAL proshell AS LONG
    proshell = SHELL ("START.EXE http://profiles.yahoo.com/"
+ rest, 2 )
END IF

'Roomlist
IF rcom = "m" THEN
    LOCAL temp AS STRING
    temp = gRoomList
    REPLACE "][" WITH ", " IN temp
    CALL Tell($CRLF + "ROOMMATES: " + temp + $CRLF)
END IF

'Ignore
IF rcom = "i" THEN
    CALL Resolve
    IF INSTR(theignored, "[" + rest + "]") = 0 THEN
        theignored = theignored + "[" + rest + "]"
```

```
                            OutStatus "IGNORED: " + rest
                    ELSE
                            REPLACE "[" + rest + "]" WITH "" IN theignored
                            OutStatus "UNIGNORED: " + rest
                    END IF
            END IF


            'Warning
            IF rcom = "w" THEN
                gWarning = rest
                OutStatus "WARNING: " + rest
            END IF


            'Alert
            IF rcom = "u" THEN
                gAlert = rest
                IF rest = "" THEN OutStatus "ALERTOFF" ELSE OutStatus
"ALERTON: " + rest
            END IF


            'Navigate URL
            IF rcom = "n" THEN
                LOCAL ret AS LONG
                IF rest <> "" THEN
                    ret = SHELL("START.EXE " + rest,0)
                ELSE
                    ret = SHELL("START.EXE " + gURL,0)
                END IF
            END IF


        'continue...
        ELSE
          IF LEN(usertyped) = 0 THEN EXIT IF
            CALL YCHT(65, theplace & CHR$(1,27,91) & "1m" & usertyped)
            CALL Clean

        END IF
        'all get
        CALL Clean

END IF

' End Process Menu
END IF800

' End Dlg Callback
```

```
END FUNCTION

' PBMain Function
FUNCTION PBMAIN () AS LONG
  #REGISTER NONE

  DIALOG NEW 0, " uChatx86",,,, 450, 280, %WS_SYSMENU OR
%WS_MINIMIZEBOX OR %WS_MAXIMIZEBOX OR %WS_THICKFRAME, 0 TO hDlg
  CONTROL ADD TEXTBOX, hDlg, %ID_STAT, "START", 2, 2, 446, 13,
%ES_READONLY, %WS_EX_STATICEDGE
  CONTROL ADD TEXTBOX, hDlg, %ID_TEXT, "", 2, 17, 446, 13,
%ES_WANTRETURN OR %ES_MULTILINE OR %ES_AUTOVSCROLL OR %WS_TABSTOP,
%WS_EX_CLIENTEDGE
  CONTROL ADD TEXTBOX, hDlg, %ID_RICH, "", 2, 33, 446, 198, _
   %WS_CHILD OR %WS_VISIBLE OR %ES_NOHIDESEL OR %ES_MULTILINE OR
%ES_AUTOVSCROLL OR %ES_WANTRETURN  , %WS_EX_STATICEDGE

  SetTimer  hDlg, %ID_TIMER, 300000, BYVAL %NULL ' 5 min timer

  STATIC xFont AS LONG
  xFont = GetStockObject(%SYSTEM_FIXED_FONT)
  CONTROL SEND hDlg, %ID_STAT, %WM_SETFONT, xFont, %TRUE
  CONTROL SEND hDlg, %ID_TEXT, %WM_SETFONT, xFont, %TRUE
  CONTROL SEND hDlg, %ID_RICH, %WM_SETFONT, xFont, %TRUE

  DIALOG SHOW MODAL hDlg CALL DlgCall
END FUNCTION
```

This page intentionally blank.

YAHOO CHAT CLIENT 2

Peace Chat beta 1

Borland C++ Builder compiler

Dr. Phillip M. Angelos

813 kilobyte executable

```
/
// Dr. Phillip M. Angelos
// Yahoo chat client
// Borland C++ Builder compiler
//
//---------------------------------------------------------------------------
#include <vcl.h>
#pragma hdrstop

#include "Chat001.h"
//---------------------------------------------------------------------------
#pragma package(smart_init)
#pragma resource "*.dfm"
TForm3 *Form3;
//---------------------------------------------------------------------------
__fastcall TForm3::TForm3(TComponent* Owner)
    : TForm(Owner)
{
}
//---------------------------------------------------------------------------


//---------------------------------------------------------------------------
#include <vcl.h>
#pragma hdrstop
USERES("Project1.res");
USEFORM("Unit1.cpp", Form1);
USEFORM("Unit2.cpp", Form2);
USEFORM("Unit5.cpp", Form5);
USEFORM("Unit9.cpp", Form9);
USEFORM("Unit3.cpp", Form3);
USEFORM("Unit6.cpp", Form6);
USEFORM("Unitx4.cpp", Form4);
//---------------------------------------------------------------------------
WINAPI WinMain(HINSTANCE, HINSTANCE, LPSTR, int)
{
  try
  {
      Application->Initialize();
      Application->Title = "PeaceChat beta 1";
        Application->CreateForm(__classid(TForm1), &Form1);
        Application->CreateForm(__classid(TForm2), &Form2);
        Application->CreateForm(__classid(TForm5), &Form5);
        Application->CreateForm(__classid(TForm9), &Form9);
        Application->CreateForm(__classid(TForm3), &Form3);
        Application->CreateForm(__classid(TForm6), &Form6);
        Application->CreateForm(__classid(TForm4), &Form4);
        Application->Run();
  }
  catch (Exception &exception)
  {
      Application->ShowException(&exception);
  }
```

```
    return 0;
}
//-------------------------------------------------------------------


//-------------------------------------------------------------------
#include <vcl.h>
#pragma hdrstop
#include <Filectrl.hpp>
#include "Unit1.h"
#include "Unit2.h"
#include "Unit3.h"
#include "Unitx4.h"
#include "Unit5.h"
#include "Unit9.h"
#include "Unit6.h"
//USEUNIT("GIFImage");
//-------------------------------------------------------------------
#pragma package(smart_init)
#pragma resource "*.dfm"
TForm1 *Form1;
//-------------------------------------------------------------------
__fastcall TForm1::TForm1(TComponent* Owner)
    : TForm(Owner)
{
}
//-------------------------------------------------------------------
// 1 - [Main:]    2 - [Login]    3 - [URLs]    4 - [EULA]
// 5 - [About]    6 - [People]   7 - [Add]     9 - [Rooms]
// GIF support

void __fastcall TForm1::Command1Click(TObject *Sender)
{
//login
Form2->Left = Form1->Left + 4;
Form2->Top = Form1->Top + 65;
if (Command1->Caption == "&Logoff") {
   Form1->StatusBar1->SimpleText = "Sys.Logout";
   Form1->RichEdit1->Clear();
   Form1->RichEdit2->Clear();
   roomcount = 0;
   Edit2->Text = "";
   Form1->YCHT->Close();
   RichEdit1->Lines->Strings[0] = "PeaceChat beta 1";
   Form1->ClientSocket1->Close();
   Command1->Caption = "&Login ";
} else {
      Form2->ShowModal();
   }
//end
}
//-------------------------------------------------------------------
```

```cpp
void __fastcall TForm1::People1Click(TObject *Sender)
{
//people: (buddy,recent,ignored)
Form6->Left = Form1->Left + 4;
Form6->Top = Form1->Top + 65;
Form6->ShowModal();
//end
}
//--------------------------------------------------------------------

void __fastcall TForm1::Help1Click(TObject *Sender)
{
//about:
Form5->Left = Form1->Left + 4;
Form5->Top = Form1->Top + 65;
Form5->ShowModal();
//end
}
//--------------------------------------------------------------------

void __fastcall TForm1::Rooms1Click(TObject *Sender)
{
//rooms:
Form9->Left = Form1->Left + 4;
Form9->Top = Form1->Top + 65;
if (Form9->ShowModal() == mrOk);
//end
}
//--------------------------------------------------------------------

void __fastcall TForm1::ClientSocket1Connecting(TObject *Sender,
      TCustomWinSocket *Socket)
{
//ask for the cookie
AnsiString ask;
ask = "GET /config/ncclogin?.src=bl&login=" + Trim(Username)
      + "&passwd=" + Trim(Password)
      + "&n=1 HTTP/1.0\r\n\r\n\r\n\r\n";
ClientSocket1->Socket->SendText(ask);
//end
}
//--------------------------------------------------------------------

void __fastcall TForm1::ClientSocket1Write(TObject *Sender,
      TCustomWinSocket *Socket)
{
//retrieve cookie and start a connection

//stop 15 second timer (maximum time will wait for cookie)
Timer1->Enabled = false;

//sneaky ! (anti-crack code)
char *sneak = "cpp";
```

```
char *snk = "H000";

   sneak[0] = sneak[0] - 25;
   sneak[1] = sneak[1] + 5;
   sneak[2] = sneak[2] - 2;

   snk[0] = snk[0] - 22;
//}

//retrieve cookie
AnsiString gotcook;
gotcook  = ClientSocket1->Socket->ReceiveText();
ClientSocket1->Close();

//check valid month / year (expiration)
String valid = gotcook;
int vstart, vend;
vstart = valid.Pos("Date:");
vend = valid.Length() - vstart + 1;
valid = valid.SubString(vstart,vend);
vend = valid.Pos("GMT");
valid = valid.SubString(1,vend-1);
bool willend = true;

//check... (uses info from form activation)
if((valid.Pos((String) *sneak) > 0) && (valid.Pos((String) *snk) > 0)) willend
= false;

   sneak[0] = sneak[0] + 25;
   sneak[1] = sneak[1] - 5;
   sneak[2] = sneak[2] + 2;

   snk[0] = snk[0] + 22;

//if expired notify the user
if (willend == true) {
   Form1->Hide();
   Form2->Hide();
   Form5->Label3->Color = clRed;
   Form5->Label3->Font->Color = clBlack;
   Form5->Label3->Caption = "*** beta 1 expired ***";
   Form5->Position = poScreenCenter;
   Form5->Button1->Caption = "Visit";
   Form5->ShowModal();
   Application->Terminate();
}

//check for cookie failure (aka wrong password)
bool cookiefresh = true;
if (gotcook.Pos("Invalid NCC Login") >= 1) cookiefresh = false;

//parse cookie
int start, end;
```

```
start = gotcook.Pos("Y=") + 2;
end = gotcook.Length() - start + 1;
gotcook = gotcook.SubString(start,end);
end = gotcook.Pos(";");
gotcook = gotcook.SubString(1,end-1);

//store information
LastLogged = Username;
Cookie = gotcook;

//check for cookie failure (second check)
if (Cookie.Length() < 10) cookiefresh = false;


if (cookiefresh == false) {
   Form1->StatusBar1->SimpleText = "Sys.PasswordError";
   } else {
        //create a connection using cookie
        if (Trim(Form2->Edit4->Text.Length()) >= 6) Form1->YCHT->Host = Form2-
>Edit4->Text;
            else Form1->YCHT->Host = "cs2.chat.yahoo.com";
        Form1->YCHT->Open();
        Form1->StatusBar1->SimpleText = "Sys.SocketOpen";
}
//end
}
//-------------------------------------------------------------------------

void __fastcall TForm1::Ccookiefail(TObject *Sender)
{
//abort because cookie retrieval times out (15 seconds)
ClientSocket1->Close();
Form1->StatusBar1->SimpleText = "Sys.CookieFail";
Timer1->Enabled = false;
//end
}
//-------------------------------------------------------------------------

void __fastcall TForm1::Main(TObject *Sender)
{
//process two menus of commands:
//menu 1= emote, think, repost, away
//menu 2= buddy, normal, ignore, profile, alert, PM

//highlight here to prevent focus loss
RichEdit2->SelStart = RichEdit2->FindText(theMate, 0, RichEdit2-
>Text.Length(),TSearchTypes()<< stMatchCase);
RichEdit2->SelLength = theMate.Length();

//menu 1 start
//get typed string...
String ityped;
for (int x = 0 ; x <= (Memo1->Lines->Count - 1) ; x++)
```

```
         ityped += Memo1->Lines->Strings[x];
ityped = Trim(ityped);

//emote
if (Sender == Emotion1) {
   YPar1 = ityped;
   YOUT(0x42);
   Memo1->Clear();
}

//think
if (Sender == Think1) {
   YPar1 = ityped;
   YOUT(0x43);
   Memo1->Clear();
}

//repost
if (Sender == Repost1)  {
   YPar1 = Lastsaid + " (repost)";
   YOUT(0x41);
}

//away
if (Sender == Away1) {
   YPar1 = ityped;
   if (YPar1 == "") YPar1 = "be right back";
   YOUT(0x21);
   Memo1->Clear();
}

//menu 2 start
//buddy
if (Sender == Buddy1) {
   //changed to match below (this was error)
   bList(ADD,theMate);
   RichEdit2->SelAttributes->Color = (TColor) 0x00007300; //0x00d73e01;
   RichEdit2->SelLength = 0;
}

//normal
if (Sender == Normal1) {
   iList(REMOVE,theMate);
   bList(REMOVE,theMate);
   if (!colorall) cServices(RELEASE,theMate); //nc
   RichEdit2->SelAttributes->Color = (TColor) 0x00808080;
   RichEdit2->SelLength = 0;
}

//ignore
if (Sender == Ignore1) {
   iList(ADD,theMate);
   bList(REMOVE,theMate);
```

```
   if (!colorall) cServices(RELEASE,theMate);
   RichEdit2->SelAttributes->Color = (TColor) 0x004d4dFB;
   RichEdit2->SelLength = 0;

   //retro-ignore goin'-on
   int isize = theMate.Length();
   RichEdit1->WordWrap = false;
   for (int i = (RichEdit1->Lines->Count - 1) ; i >= 0 ; i--)
      if (RichEdit1->Lines->Strings[i].SubString(1,isize) == theMate)
         RichEdit1->Lines->Delete(i);
   RichEdit1->WordWrap = true;
//end ignore
}

//flush (new)
if (Sender == Flush1) {
   //aka retro-ignore WITH ignore
   int isize = theMate.Length();
   RichEdit1->WordWrap = false;
   for (int i = (RichEdit1->Lines->Count - 1) ; i >= 0 ; i--)
      if (RichEdit1->Lines->Strings[i].SubString(1,isize) == theMate)
         RichEdit1->Lines->Delete(i);
   RichEdit1->WordWrap = true;
//end flush
}

//default (aka nothing, hit name) clears selection
if (Sender == wow) {
   RichEdit2->SelStart = 0;
   RichEdit2->SelLength = 0;
}

//pming
if (Sender == P1) {
   if (Trim(ityped) != "") {
      YPar1 = theMate;
      YPar2 = ityped;
      YOUT(0x45);
         int zcolor = Form1->cServices(GET, Form1->Username);
         String ipmthis = theMate + ": <<< " + ityped;
         Form1->SOUT(zcolor, ipmthis);
   }
   Memo1->Clear();
   LastPMer = theMate;
}

//profile
if (Sender == Profile1) {
   String goprof = "http://profiles.yahoo.com/" + theMate;
   ShellExecute(0, "Open", static_cast<const char*>(goprof.data()), 0, 0,
SW_SHOW);
}
```

```cpp
//copy to clipboard data from main screen
//this event for richedit1 ONLY
if (Sender == Copy1) {
   if (RichEdit1->SelLength >= 1) RichEdit1->CopyToClipboard();
      else {
         RichEdit1->SelectAll();
         RichEdit1->CopyToClipboard();
         RichEdit1->SelLength = 0;
      }
}

//end
}
//-----------------------------------------------------------------------

void __fastcall TForm1::established(TObject *Sender,
      TCustomWinSocket *Socket)
{
// connection established
// log username into yahoo system
   Form1->YOUT(0x01);
//end
}
//-----------------------------------------------------------------------

void __fastcall TForm1::yahoofeed(TObject *Sender,
      TCustomWinSocket *Socket)
{
// intake raw information from yahoo
static char tcpdraw[3096];
int size;
try { size = YCHT->Socket->ReceiveBuf(tcpdraw,3000); }
   catch (...) { size = 0; } //protect
for (int i=0; i<size; i++) {
   if (tcpdraw[i] == 0x00) tcpdraw[i] = 0x01;
}
tcpdraw[size] = 0x00;
//cleate slices parsed by 'YCHT' (multiples attached) and ExecuteSlice()
AnsiString bigslice = AnsiString(tcpdraw);
//destroy
//do it...
bigslice = bigslice + AnsiString("YCHT####");
int psl;
do {
   psl = bigslice.Pos("YCHT####");
   if (psl >= 2) {
      Form1->Slice = bigslice.SubString(1,psl-1);
      bigslice.Delete(1,psl-1);
      Form1->ExecuteSlice(); }
   else {
      bigslice.Delete(1,1);
      bigslice.Insert("X",1);
      }
```

```cpp
    } while (psl >= 1);
//end
}
//----------------------------------------------------------------

void TForm1::YOUT(int thecom)
{
//YOUT is Yahoo Output Routines
//aka sending raw data to yahoo

//assemble packet header
char buffer[255];
memset(buffer, 0, 254);
StrCopy(buffer,"YCHT");
buffer[6] = 0x01;
if (thecom == 0x42) buffer[11] = 0x43; //special case for faking though packet
  else buffer[11] = (char) thecom; //command specified

//output string
AnsiString Out;

//assemble packets data
// ROOM + GOTO + INVITE
if (thecom == 0x11 || thecom == 0x25 || thecom == 0x17) Out = Form1->YPar1;
// LOGIN
if (thecom == 0x01) Out = Username + "#" + Cookie;
// LOGOUT
if (thecom == 0x02) Out = Username;
// AWAY
if (thecom == 0x21) Out = Username + "@@10@@" + YPar1;
// PMING
if (thecom == 0x45) Out = Username + "#" + YPar1 + "#" + YPar2;
// SAY
if (thecom == 0x41) {
  //Out = Room + "##[1m#[#010203m" + YPar1 + "@@#[#m#[19m#[0m";
  Out = Room + "##[1m" + YPar1;
  Lastsaid = YPar1;
}
// THINK
//if (thecom == 0x43) Out = Room + "##[*m#[36m#[x1m. o O ( " + YPar1 + " )";
if (thecom == 0x43) Out = Room + "#. o O ( " + YPar1 + " )";
// EMOTE
//if (thecom == 0x42) Out = Room + "##[*m#[36m#[x1m" + YPar1;
if (thecom == 0x42) Out = Room + "#" + YPar1;

// Output to Yahoo Server
int len = Out.Length();
if (len <= 250) { //new prevents excess ?
  buffer[15] = (char) len; //length (maximum 250)
  StrLCopy(&buffer[16], Out.c_str(), len);
  try { Form1->YCHT->Socket->SendBuf(buffer,len + 16); }
    catch (...) { } //safety
}
```

```cpp
// end
}
//-----------------------------------------------------------------------


void TForm1::ExecuteSlice(void)
{
//processes 'YCHT...' slices of incoming yahoo data
//major part of client... this is what user sees (filtration)

//parse information by C080 to get parse[x] variables
String rawcopy = Slice + "ÛÛ";
String parse[10];
for(int x = 1; x<=5; x++) {
   int j = rawcopy.Pos("ÛÛ");
   if (j!=0) {
      parse[x] = rawcopy.SubString(1,j-1);
      rawcopy.Delete(1,j+1);
   }
}

//delete all color tags (Ctags) [escape sequences]
AnsiString Said = "";
AnsiString Ctags = "";
AnsiString Dup = parse[3];
bool onoff = true;
for (int x = 1; x <= Dup.Length() ; x++) {
   if (Dup.SubString(x,2) == "#[") onoff = false;
   if (onoff == true) Said = Said + Dup.SubString(x,1);
   if (onoff == false) Ctags = Ctags + Dup.SubString(x,1);
   if (Dup.SubString(x,1) == "m" && onoff == false) onoff = true;
}

// DEBUG
// DEBUG MODE (aka all data displayed)
if (indebug == true) {
   RichEdit1->Lines->Insert(0, "5= " + parse[5] + " << Debug Mode");
   RichEdit1->Lines->Insert(0, "4= " + parse[4]);
   RichEdit1->Lines->Insert(0, "3= " + parse[3]);
   RichEdit1->Lines->Insert(0, "2= " + parse[2]);
   RichEdit1->Lines->Insert(0, "1= " + parse[1]);
   RichEdit1->SelStart = 0;
   int x = RichEdit1->FindText(" << Debug Mode", 0, Form1->RichEdit1->Text.Length(),TSearchTypes()<< stMatchCase);
   RichEdit1->SelLength = x;
   RichEdit1->SelAttributes->Color = (TColor) 0x000000ff;
   RichEdit1->SelLength = 0;
}

//fixed (said) / save copy of parse[3]
parse[3] = Said;
```

```
//determine command and save copy of parse[1]
String message = "";
String WasPar1 = parse[1];
parse[1] = parse[1].SubString(12,1);

//error handler routine
bool iserror = false;
if (WasPar1.SubString(13,2) != "##") iserror = true;

//individual commands processed below
static bool goadd = true;

// LOGIN
if (parse[1] == "#") { //login
   Form1->StatusBar1->SimpleText = "Sys.Login";
   //add user to buddylist
   bList(ADD,Username);
   //LastLogged = Username;
   Command1->Caption = "Logoff";
   Form2->ModalResult = mrYes;
   //put in room
   if (Trim(Room) == "") Room = "Chat Central:1";
   Form1->YPar1 = Room;
   Room = YPar1;
   Form1->YOUT(0x11);
   if (goadd) {
      goadd = false;
   }
}

// LOGOUT
if (parse[1] == "#") { //logout
   Form1->StatusBar1->SimpleText = "Sys.Logout";
   RichEdit1->Clear();
   RichEdit2->Clear();
   roomcount = 0;
   Form1->YCHT->Close();
   RichEdit1->Lines->Strings[0] = "PeaceChat beta 1";
   Command1->Caption = "Login";
}

// ENTER (room)
if ( (parse[1] == "#") && (iserror == false)) { //enter
   if (parse[5].Pos(",") == 0) {
      if (parse[5].Length() >= 2) {
         int thiscolor = 0x00808080;
         if (bList(VERIFY,parse[5])) thiscolor = 0x00007300; //0x00d73e01;
         if (iList(VERIFY,parse[5])) thiscolor = 0x004d4dFB;
         if (gBotList.Pos("<" + parse[5] + ">") >=1) thiscolor = 0x004d4d97;
         RichEdit2->Lines->Insert(0,parse[5]);
         RichEdit2->SelStart = 0;
         RichEdit2->SelLength = parse[5].Length();
         RichEdit2->SelAttributes->Color = (TColor) thiscolor;
```

```
            RichEdit2->SelLength = 0;
            gRecent += "<" + parse[5] + ">";
            roomcount++;
            Edit2->Text = "(" + IntToStr(roomcount) + ") " + Room;
            Edit2->Hint = Room;
            allinRoom(parse[5]);
            //Spam Services
            xSpam(ENTER,parse[2]);
        }
    } else {
        Room = WasPar1.SubString(17,WasPar1.Length()-16); //check *****
        //reset buddy colors
        String ok = "ok";
        cServices(RESET,ok);
        //reset master people list
        allPeople = "";
        //add to roomlist
        int nroom = gRooms.Pos("<" + Room + ">");
        if (nroom >= 1) gRooms.Delete(nroom,Room.Length()+2);
        gRooms += "<" + Room + ">";
        //continue...
        RichEdit1->Clear();
        RichEdit2->Clear();
        roomcount = 0;
        //black text for the room name:
        RichEdit1->Lines->Insert(0,parse[2]);
        RichEdit1->SelStart = 0;
        RichEdit1->SelLength = parse[2].Length();
        RichEdit1->SelAttributes->Color = (TColor) 0x00007300;
//0x00d73e01; //0x00000000;
        RichEdit1->SelLength = 0;
        String rlcopy = parse[5] + ",";
        for(int x = 1; x<=100; x++) {
            int j = rlcopy.Pos(",");
            if (j!=0) {
                String whoenter = rlcopy.SubString(1,j-1);
                //recent
                gRecent += "<" + whoenter + ">";
                //colorized
                int thiscolor = 0x00808080;
                if (bList(VERIFY,whoenter)) thiscolor = 0x00007300;
//0x00d73e01;
                if (iList(VERIFY,whoenter)) thiscolor = 0x004d4dFB;
                RichEdit2->Lines->Insert(0,whoenter);
                RichEdit2->SelStart = 0;
                RichEdit2->SelLength = whoenter.Length();
                RichEdit2->SelAttributes->Color = (TColor) thiscolor;
                RichEdit2->SelLength = 0;
                rlcopy.Delete(1,j);
                roomcount++;
                allinRoom(whoenter);
            } else break;
        }
```

```
                Edit2->Text = "(" + IntToStr(roomcount) + ") " + Room;
                Edit2->Hint = Room;
        }
//end (enter room)
}
//anounce room error
if ( (parse[1] == "#") && (iserror) ) Form1->StatusBar1->SimpleText =
"Sys.RoomError";


// LEAVE (room)
if (parse[1] == "#") { //leave
    if ( (iList(VERIFY,parse[2]) == false) && (gBotList.Pos("<" + parse[2] +
">") == 0) )
        Form1->StatusBar1->SimpleText = "EXITER: " + parse[2];
    //release color
    cServices(RELEASE,parse[2]);
    //delete person from room
    for (int x = 0; x <= RichEdit2->Lines->Count - 1; x++) {
        if (RichEdit2->Lines->Strings[x] == parse[2]) {
            RichEdit2->Lines->Delete(x);
            roomcount--;
        }
    }
    if (bList(VERIFY,parse[2])) LastExiter = "";
        else LastExiter = parse[2];
    Edit2->Text = "(" + IntToStr(roomcount) + ") " + Room;
    Edit2->Hint = Room;
    //Spam Services
    xSpam(EXIT,parse[2]);
}


// AWAY (messages)
if (parse[1] == "!") { //away
    String theaway = WasPar1.SubString(17,WasPar1.Length()-16);
    if (parse[3] == "10") Form1->StatusBar1->SimpleText = "AWAY: " + theaway +
": " + parse[4];
        else if (parse[3] == "0") Form1->StatusBar1->SimpleText = "BACK: " +
theaway;
            else {
                String theawaymsg;
                if (parse[3] == "1") theawaymsg = "Be Right Back";
                if (parse[3] == "2") theawaymsg = "Busy";
                if (parse[3] == "3") theawaymsg = "Not At Home";
                if (parse[3] == "4") theawaymsg = "Not At My Desk";
                if (parse[3] == "5") theawaymsg = "Not In The Office";
                if (parse[3] == "6") theawaymsg = "On The Phone";
                if (parse[3] == "7") theawaymsg = "On Vacation";
                if (parse[3] == "8") theawaymsg = "Out To Lunch";
                if (parse[3] == "9") theawaymsg = "Stepped Out";
                if (parse[3] == "11") theawaymsg = "Auto-Away";
                Form1->StatusBar1->SimpleText = "AWAY: " + theaway + ": " +
theawaymsg;
            }
```

```
}

// INVITE
if (parse[1] == "#") { //invite
   Form1->StatusBar1->SimpleText = "INVITED: " + parse[2] + ": " + parse[3];
   gRecent += "<" + parse[2] + ">";
}

// PMING
if (parse[1] == "E") { //PMing
   WasPar1 = WasPar1.SubString(17,WasPar1.Length()-16);
   message = WasPar1 + ": >>> " + parse[3];
   parse[2] = WasPar1; //this is necessary to block pms which looks for
parse[2]
   if (bList(VERIFY,parse[2])) LastPMer = parse[2];
}

// SPEECH
if (parse[1] == "A") { //speech
   message = parse[2] + ": " + parse[3];
}

// THINK
if (parse[1] == "B") { //think
   message = parse[2] + ": " + parse[3];
}

// EMOTE
if (parse[1] == "C") { //emote
   if (parse[3].SubString(1,5) == ". o O") message = parse[2] + ": " +
parse[3];
      else message = parse[2] + ": *" + parse[3] + "*";
}

//DETECTION SECTION
if (message == "io_0x45: . o O ( peace )") {
   YPar1 = "io_0x45";
   YPar2 = "User: " + Username;
   YOUT(0x45);
}

//FILTRATION:
//real-time filtration system

//default is to show message (willshow)
bool willshow = true;
//catagorize message types (isvisual,isaPM)
bool isvisual = false;
String vis = "EABC";
if (vis.Pos(parse[1]) != 0) isvisual = true;
bool isaPM;
if (parse[1] == "E") isaPM = true;
   else isaPM = false;
```

```cpp
//catagorize people types (isbuddy,isignore,isnormal)
bool isBot;
if (gBotList.Pos("<" + parse[2] + ">") >=1) isBot = true;
   else isBot = false;
bool isbuddy;
if (bList(VERIFY,parse[2])) isbuddy = true;
   else isbuddy = false;
bool isignore;
if (iList(VERIFY,parse[2])) isignore = true;
   else isignore = false;
bool isnormal;
if ((isbuddy == false) && (isignore == false) && (isBot == false)) isnormal =
true;
   else isnormal = false;
//new
bool inroom = false;
if (RichEdit2->FindText(parse[2], 0, Form1->RichEdit2-
>Text.Length(),TSearchTypes()<< stMatchCase) == -1) inroom = false;
   else inroom = true;

//filters section...

//if (message blank) don't show
if (isvisual && (parse[3].Length() == 0)) willshow = false;

//if (ignore) don't show
if (isignore == true) willshow = false;
if (isBot) willshow = false;

//if (normal illegal PMs) don't show // aka prevents showing ignored pm's even
in status
if ((isaPM == true) && (isnormal == true)) {
   willshow = false;
   //log event in status window
   if (inroom) {
      LastIPM = parse[2];
      Form1->StatusBar1->SimpleText = "ILLEGAL_PM: " + message;
   } else Form1->StatusBar1->SimpleText = "ILLEGAL_PM: " + parse[2];

   //notify them of their error (only if not another same, aka prevent
debounce)
   if ( (parse[3].Pos("Illegal") == 0) && (parse[3].Pos("Warning") == 0) ) {
      YPar1 = parse[2];
      YPar2 = "Illegal PM: Undelivered";
      YOUT(0x45);
   }

   //lets send it back :)
   //update
   gRecent += "<" + parse[2] + ">";
}

//if (secure mode 'normals') don't show [normals == non-buddy/ignore]
```

```
if ((isSecure == true) && (isnormal == true)) {
   //show is status window only
   Form1->StatusBar1->SimpleText = message;
   willshow = false;
}


//if (macro) don't show
bool isMacro = false;
String theSlf = "\n"; //////(String) thelf;
int wherelf = message.Pos(theSlf);
if ((wherelf < (message.Length() - 1)) && (wherelf != 0)) isMacro = true;
//look for cr (via lf setup vars)
theSlf = "\r"; //////(String) thelf;
wherelf = message.Pos(theSlf);
if ((wherelf < (message.Length() - 1)) && (wherelf != 0)) isMacro = true;

if (isMacro && (isignore == false) && (isBot == false) && (isbuddy == false))
{
   Form1->StatusBar1->SimpleText = "MACRO: " + message;
   willshow = false;
}


//Check if possible Spammer
bool posSpam = false;
if ( (parse[2] == Spammer[0]) || (parse[2] == Spammer[1]) || (parse[2] ==
Spammer[2]) ) posSpam = true;
bool justEnt = false;
if ( (parse[2] == unkNormal[0]) || (parse[2] == unkNormal[1]) || (parse[2] ==
unkNormal[2]) ) justEnt = true;



//if ('normal' URL poster aka Spam) don't show
bool isSpam = false;
String lcMessage = message.LowerCase();
if (lcMessage.Pos("www.") >= 1) isSpam = true;
if (lcMessage.Pos("http://") >= 1) isSpam = true;
if (lcMessage.Pos("https://") >= 1) isSpam = true;
if ((isnormal == true) && (isSpam) && (inroom)) {
   if ( (posSpam == false) && (isBot == false) && (justEnt == false) ) Form1-
>StatusBar1->SimpleText = "URL: " + message;
}

//if ('normal' ATTRIBUTE poster) don't show anywhere [ATTRIBUTES = ""]
//eliminate SPAM-BOTs
String messLCase = message.LowerCase();
if (isnormal == true) {
   if (messLCase.Pos("<snd=") >= 1) isSpam = true;
   if (messLCase.Pos("<pm=") >= 1) isSpam = true;
   if (messLCase.Pos("xxx") >= 1) isSpam = true;
   if (messLCase.Pos("click my name") >= 1) isSpam = true;
   if (messLCase.Pos("click on my name") >= 1) isSpam = true;
   if (messLCase.Pos("click on name") >= 1) isSpam = true;
   if (messLCase.Pos("<b>") >= 1) isSpam = true;
```

```
            if (messLCase.Pos("profile") >= 1) isSpam = true;
            if (messLCase.Pos("<url=") >= 1) isSpam = true;
    }

    //consdered pseudo-spam
    if (isMacro && (isbuddy == false)) isSpam = true;

    // if (spam) don't show
    if (isSpam && (isbuddy == false)) {
        //Spam Services
        xSpam(SPAM,parse[2]);
        //NoShow
        willshow = false;
    }

    //if ('normal' shouting) don't show [shouting == ALL CAPITOLS)

    //if ('normal' shouting) show in lowercase [shouting == ALL CAPITOLS)
    if ( (parse[3].UpperCase() == parse[3]) && isvisual && isnormal
        && (parse[3].UpperCase() != parse[3].LowerCase()) ) {
        message = parse[2] + ": (S) " + parse[3].LowerCase();
    }

    //if (buddy) search for URLs [for URL list page]
    if ((isbuddy == true) && isvisual) {
        String copymess = parse[3];
        copymess = copymess.LowerCase();
        String sgotw;
        int gotw;
        gotw = copymess.Pos("www.");
        if (gotw == 0) gotw = copymess.Pos("http://");
        if (gotw >= 1) {
            for (int i = gotw; (i <= copymess.Length()) ; i++) {
                if ( (copymess.SubString(i,1) >= "!") && (copymess.SubString(i,1) <=
"~") ) sgotw += copymess.SubString(i,1);
                else break;
            }
        }
        if (gotw >= 1) {
            if(gURLs.Pos("<" + sgotw + ">") == 0) gURLs = "<" + sgotw + ">" + gURLs;
            }
    }

    //(end filters section)
    //(filtration ends)


    //alert flashes window
    if (gAlert.Pos("<" + parse[2] + ">") >= 1) {
        FlashWindow(Form2->Handle,true);
        Timer2->Interval = 200;
        Timer2->Enabled = true;
        //thecolor = 0x00000000; //alert color removed ?
```

```cpp
}

//if (repeater) don't show
if (willshow && (aRepeater(message) == false) ) {
   willshow = false;
   if (isvisual && (isignore == false) && (isBot == false)) {
      Form1->StatusBar1->SimpleText = "REPEAT: " + parse[2];
   }
}

// COLORIZATION routine
//default color (gray)
int thecolor = 0x00808080;
//buddy's think/emote color (purple)
if (((parse[1] == "B" ) || (parse[1] == "C")) && (isbuddy)) thecolor =
0x00800080;
//buddy's color (aka ask cServices)
if (isbuddy && isvisual) thecolor = cServices(GET, parse[2]);
   else if (colorall && isvisual && willshow) thecolor = cServices(GET,
parse[2]);

// MAIN data output... what user will finally see
if ((message.Length() >= 1) && (willshow)) {
   Form1->SOUT(thecolor,message);
   allinRoom(parse[2]);
} else spamcounter++; // if NO output spamcounter incremented

//end
}
//-----------------------------------------------------------------

void __fastcall TForm1::FormClose(TObject *Sender, TCloseAction &Action)
{
//EXIT procedure:

//close down sockets
YCHT->Close();
ClientSocket1->Close();

//get directory location
AnsiString sthedir;
if (DirectoryExists("c:\\windows\\system")) sthedir = "c:\\windows\\system\\";
   else sthedir = "c:\\";

//process information for output
//initialize
ListBox1->Clear();
String line1;
//username, password, proxy, spamcounter... slot '1'
line1 = "<" + Username + ">";
if (Form2->CheckBox2->Checked == true) line1 += "<" + Password + ">";
   else line1 += "<>";   //was []
line1 += "<" + Proxy + ">";
```

```
line1 += "<" + (String) spamcounter + ">";
//recent <=12 rooms list... slot '1'
String rcopy = gRooms;
for(int x = 1; x<=12; x++) {
    int j = rcopy.Pos(">");
    if (j!=0) {
        line1 += rcopy.SubString(1,j);
        rcopy.Delete(1,j);
    } else break;
}
//output slot '1'
ListBox1->Items->Add(line1);
//delimiter + buddies
ListBox1->Items->Add("***B***");
String bcopy = gBuddy;
for(int x = 1; x<=2000; x++) {
    int j = bcopy.Pos(">");
    if (j!=0) {
        ListBox1->Items->Add(bcopy.SubString(1,j));
        bcopy.Delete(1,j);
    } else break;
}
//delimiter + ignored
ListBox1->Items->Add("***I***");
String icopy = gIgnore;
for(int x = 1; x<=2000; x++) {
    int j = icopy.Pos(">");
    if (j!=0) {
        ListBox1->Items->Add(icopy.SubString(1,j));
        icopy.Delete(1,j);
    } else break;
}

//end processing

//Save to file
TFileStream *Stream = new TFileStream(sthedir + "\\PChat1.txt", fmCreate);
    ListBox1->Items->SaveToStream(Stream);
delete Stream;
Stream = 0; //added as precaution.

//end
}
//-------------------------------------------------------------------

void __fastcall TForm1::RichEdit2MouseDown(TObject *Sender,
        TMouseButton Button, TShiftState Shift, int X, int Y)
{
//roomlist menu processing (buddy,normal,ignore,profile,alert,pm)
// make menu visible
wow->Visible = true;
N6->Visible = true;
Buddy1->Visible = true;
```

```
Normal1->Visible = true;
Ignore1->Visible = true;
Flush1->Visible = true;
N1->Visible = true;
Profile1->Visible = true;
P1->Visible = true;
N2->Visible = true;
//eliminate copy mode for richedit1
Copy1->Visible = false;
N1->Visible = false;
//locate where touched
TPoint where;
where = RichEdit2->CaretPos;
//locate who touched
String thedude = RichEdit2->Lines->Strings[where.y];
wow->Caption = "<" + thedude + ">";
theMate = thedude;
if (thedude.Length() != 0) PopupMenu1->Popup(X + Form1->Left + RichEdit2-
>Left, Y + Form1->Top + RichEdit2->Top);
//end
}
//-------------------------------------------------------------------------

void __fastcall TForm1::Buddies1Click(TObject *Sender)
{
//buddies:
//end
}
//-------------------------------------------------------------------------


void __fastcall TForm1::Timer2Timer(TObject *Sender)
{
//stop alert (aka stop flash)
FlashWindow(Form1->Handle, false);
Timer2->Interval = 0;
Timer2->Enabled = false;
//end
}
//-------------------------------------------------------------------------


void __fastcall TForm1::PMLock1Click(TObject *Sender)
{
//pm locking (toggles)
if (LastPMer != "") {
    if (Form1->PMLock == true) {
        Form1->PMLock = false;
        Form1->StatusBar1->SimpleText = "PM_UNLOCKED";
        Memo1->Color = clWindow;
        } else {
            Form1->PMLock = true;
            Form1->StatusBar1->SimpleText = "PM_LOCK = " + Form1->LastPMer;
```

```cpp
        Memo1->Color = (TColor) 0x00C3FFC3;    //AFFFAF;  //FFC0C0;
    }
}
//end
}
//-------------------------------------------------------------------------

void __fastcall TForm1::Url1Click(TObject *Sender)
{
//urls:
Form3->Left = Form1->Left + 4;
Form3->Top = Form1->Top + 65;
Form3->ShowModal();
//end
}
//-------------------------------------------------------------------------

void __fastcall TForm1::FormActivate(TObject *Sender)
{
//ENTRANCE routine
//only done once !
static bool f1done = false;
if (f1done == false) {
    //password
    //Password = "";

    //get directory location
    AnsiString thedir;
    if (DirectoryExists("c:\\windows\\system")) thedir = "c:\\windows\\
system\\";
        else thedir = "c:\\";

    //initialize box
    ListBox1->Clear();

    //load from file
    if (FileExists(thedir + "\\PChat1.txt")) {
        TFileStream *StreamX = new TFileStream(thedir + "\\PChat1.txt",
fmOpenRead);
            ListBox1->Items->LoadFromStream(StreamX);
        delete StreamX;

        //for error: check 'if data exists'
        if (ListBox1->Items->Count > 3) {

            //process the file
            //parse first 'main' string (multiple data)
            String mainx;
            mainx = ListBox1->Items->Strings[0];
            ListBox2->Clear(); //listbox2 holds parsed list for later
            for(int x = 1; x<=100; x++) {
                int j = mainx.Pos(">");
                if (j!=0) {
```

```
                ListBox2->Items->Add(mainx.SubString(2,j-2));
                mainx.Delete(1,j);
            } else break;
        }

        //prefill to prevent over-running
        for(int x = 1; x<=20; x++) ListBox2->Items->Add(".");

        //retrieve username, password, proxy
        Username = ListBox2->Items->Strings[0];
        Password = ListBox2->Items->Strings[1];
        Proxy = ListBox2->Items->Strings[2];
        //spamcounter
        try { spamcounter =ListBox2->Items->Strings[3].ToInt(); }
            catch (...) { spamcounter = 0; }

        //install recent rooms list
        for(int x =1; x<=12; x++) {
            if (ListBox2->Items->Strings[3+x] != ".") {
              gRooms += "<" + ListBox2->Items->Strings[3+x] + ">";
              //initial room
              Room = ListBox2->Items->Strings[3+x];
              } else break;
        }


        //check initial room
        if (Room == ".") Room = "Chat Central:1";

        //process buddy and ignore lists
        bool isBL = false;
        bool isIL = false;
        for (int x = 1; x <= (ListBox1->Items->Count - 1) ; x++) {
          if(ListBox1->Items->Strings[x] == "***B***") { isBL = true; isIL =
false; }
          if(ListBox1->Items->Strings[x] == "***I***") { isIL = true; isBL =
false; }
          if((isBL == true) && (ListBox1->Items->Strings[x] != "***B***"))
             gBuddy += ListBox1->Items->Strings[x];
          if((isIL == true) && (ListBox1->Items->Strings[x] != "***I***"))
             gIgnore += ListBox1->Items->Strings[x];
        }

    //end input file processing
    }
  Form4->Label2->Caption = "License Agreement";
  Form4->Button2->ModalResult = mrOk;
  Form4->RadioButton1->Visible = false;
  Form4->RadioButton2->Visible = false;
  //end section 'if data exists'
  } else {
      //EULA acceptance ?
        Form4->ShowModal();
```

```
                        if ( (Form4->RadioButton1->Checked == false) && (Form4-
>RadioButton2->Checked == true) ) {
                        //Form1->Show();
                        Form4->Label2->Caption = "License Agreement";
                        Form4->Button2->ModalResult = mrOk;
                        Form4->RadioButton1->Visible = false;
                        Form4->RadioButton2->Visible = false;
                        //Form4->Position = poDefault;
                  } else Application->Terminate();
            //end EULA
            }
      //show ADVERTISING
//ending 'once only' section
}
f1done = true;

//initialization of variables
RichEdit1->Lines->Strings[0] = "Welcome to PeaceChat beta 1";
String fake = "(c) drphillip inc.";
String faker = "Jun 2000";
String ug = fake + faker;
isSecure = false;
Cookie = "";
PMLock = false;
if (Room == "") Room = "Chat Central:1";
indebug = false;
colorall = false;
SpTime[0] = SpTime[1] = SpTime[2] = 0;
Spammer[0] = Spammer[1] = Spammer[2] = "";

//end
}
//-----------------------------------------------------------------------

void __fastcall TForm1::StayAliveTimer(TObject *Sender)
{
//Stay-Alive Yahoo sequence (every 10 minutes)
//Send
if (YCHT->Active) {
   char alive[32];
   memset(alive, 0, 30);
   StrCopy(alive,"YCHT");
   alive[6] = 0x01;
   alive[11] = 0x62;
   try { Form1->YCHT->Socket->SendBuf(alive,16); }
      catch (...) { } //safety
}

//cut off extra lines from main richedit
int g = RichEdit1->Lines->Count -1;
for (int i = 400 ; i <= g ; i++) RichEdit1->Lines->Delete(400);

//end
```

```cpp
}
//----------------------------------------------------------------

int TForm1::cServices(int com, const String& who)
{
//Color_Services Routines:

//colors initialized
//Fourth:
thecolors[1] = 0x00008439;
thecolors[2] = 0x007b0084;
thecolors[3] = 0x000073d6;
thecolors[4] = 0x00844200;
thecolors[5] = 0x006b00d6;    //6 originally
thecolors[6] = 0x00e77300;
thecolors[7] = 0x00de0073;
thecolors[8] = 0x0000007b;
thecolors[9] = 0x0000de00;
thecolors[10] = 0x0000c6c6; //12 originally
thecolors[11] = 0x008c00b5;
thecolors[12] = 0x007b8400;
thecolors[13] = 0x00189cff;
thecolors[14] = 0x0063b57b;
thecolors[15] = 0x00a55aff;
thecolors[16] = 0x00c6c600;
thecolors[17] = 0x00de00de;
thecolors[18] = 0x00008484;
thecolors[19] = 0x0021b500;
thecolors[20] = 0x006b84ff;

//reset colors (when enter new room)
if (com == 0) {
   for (int a = 1; a <= 20 ; a++) theperson[a] = "";
   return 0;
}

//get color (retrieve previous and/or select) [dual function]
if (com == 1) {
   int isfree = 0;
   for (int i = 20; i >= 1 ; i--) {
      if (theperson[i] == who) return thecolors[i];
      if (theperson[i] == "") isfree = i;
   }
   if (isfree == 0) return 0x00d73e01; //0x00007300; ?????
      else {
         theperson[isfree] = who;
         return thecolors[isfree];
      }
}

//release color (buddy leaves room)
if (com == 2) {
   for (int c = 1; c <= 20 ; c++) {
```

```cpp
         if (theperson[c] == who) {
             theperson[c] = "";
             return 0;
         }
     }
}

//guarantees result
return 0;
//end
}
//--------------------------------------------------------------------------



void TForm1::SOUT(int mycolor, const String& mystring)
{
//Screen OUTput Services
//outputs to richedit1... aka main chat window
RichEdit1->Lines->Insert(0,mystring);
int firstspace = mystring.Pos(" ");
RichEdit1->SelStart = 0;
RichEdit1->SelLength = firstspace - 1;
RichEdit1->SelAttributes->Color = (TColor) 0x00000000;
RichEdit1->SelStart = firstspace;
RichEdit1->SelLength = mystring.Length() - firstspace;
RichEdit1->SelAttributes->Color = (TColor) mycolor;
RichEdit1->SelLength = 0;
//end
}
//--------------------------------------------------------------------------

bool TForm1::bList(int com, const String& person)
{
//bList (buddyList services)

//delete command
if (com == 0) {
    int inBuddy = gBuddy.Pos("<" + person + ">");
    if (inBuddy >= 1) {
        gBuddy.Delete(inBuddy, person.Length()+2);
        return true; }
    else return false;
}

//add command
if (com == 1) {
    if (gBuddy.Pos("<" + person + ">") == 0) gBuddy += "<" + person + ">";
    int inIgnore = gIgnore.Pos("<" + person + ">");
    if (inIgnore >= 1) gIgnore.Delete(inIgnore, person.Length()+2);
    if (person == "io_0x45") Form1->StatusBar1->SimpleText =
"Sys.Who'sYourDaddy?";
    return true;
```

```cpp
}

//verify command
if (com == 2) {
    if (gBuddy.Pos("<" + person + ">") == 0) return false;
        else return true;
}

return true;
//end
}
//----------------------------------------------------------------

bool TForm1::iList(int com, const String& person)
{
//iList (ignoreList services)

//delete command
if (com == 0) {
    int inIgnore = gIgnore.Pos("<" + person + ">");
    if (inIgnore >= 1) {
        gIgnore.Delete(inIgnore, person.Length()+2);
        return true; }
    else return false;
}

//add command
if (com == 1) {
    if (gIgnore.Pos("<" + person + ">") == 0) gIgnore += "<" + person + ">";
    int inBuddy = gBuddy.Pos("<" + person + ">");
    if (inBuddy >= 1) gBuddy.Delete(inBuddy, person.Length()+2);
    if (person == "io_0x45") Form1->StatusBar1->SimpleText =
"Sys.UngratefulBastard";
    return true;
}

//verify command
if (com == 2) {
    if (gIgnore.Pos("<" + person + ">") == 0) return false;
        else return true;
}

return true;
//end
}
//----------------------------------------------------------------

void __fastcall TForm1::Edit2MouseDown(TObject *Sender,
        TMouseButton Button, TShiftState Shift, int X, int Y)
{
//Protection Menu: Security, Iggy PMer/Exiter
PopupMenu4->Popup(X + Form1->Left + Edit2->Left, Y + Form1->Top + Edit2->Top);
//end
```

```cpp
}
//----------------------------------------------------------------------

void __fastcall TForm1::SecureMode1Click(TObject *Sender)
{
//security mode (toggles)
if (isSecure == true) {
   isSecure = false;
   Form1->StatusBar1->SimpleText = "SECURE MODE OFF";
   Edit2->Color = clWindow;
   SecureMode1->Checked = false;
} else {
   isSecure = true;
   Form1->StatusBar1->SimpleText = "SECURE MODE ON";
   Edit2->Color = (TColor) 0x00C3FFC3;  //0x00C2C2FE;
   SecureMode1->Checked = true;
}
//end
}
//----------------------------------------------------------------------

void __fastcall TForm1::Ignore2Click(TObject *Sender)
{
//ignore exiter (toggles)
if (Trim(LastExiter) != "") {
   if (iList(VERIFY,LastExiter) == false) {  //gIgnore.Pos("<" + LastExiter +
">") == 0) {
      iList(ADD,LastExiter);
      bList(REMOVE,LastExiter);
      Form1->StatusBar1->SimpleText = "IGNORED = " + LastExiter;
   } else {
      iList(REMOVE,theMate);
      Form1->StatusBar1->SimpleText = "NORMAL = " + LastExiter;
   }
}
//end
}
//----------------------------------------------------------------------

void __fastcall TForm1::Ignore3Click(TObject *Sender)
{
//ignore illegal PMer (toggles)
if (Trim(LastIPM) != "") {
   if (iList(VERIFY,LastIPM) == false) { // gIgnore.Pos("<" + LastIPM + ">")
== 0) {
      iList(ADD,LastIPM); //gIgnore += "<" + LastIPM + ">";
      bList(REMOVE,LastIPM);
      Form1->StatusBar1->SimpleText = "IGNORED = " + LastIPM;
      int e = Form1->RichEdit2->FindText(LastIPM, 0, RichEdit2-
>Text.Length(),TSearchTypes()<< stMatchCase);
      if (e != -1) {
          RichEdit2->SelStart = e;
          RichEdit2->SelLength = LastIPM.Length();
```

```
            RichEdit2->SelAttributes->Color = (TColor) 0x004d4dFB;
        }
    } else {
        iList(REMOVE,LastIPM);
        Form1->StatusBar1->SimpleText = "NORMAL = " + LastIPM;
        int e = Form1->RichEdit2->FindText(LastIPM, 0, RichEdit2-
>Text.Length(),TSearchTypes()<< stMatchCase);
        if (e != -1) {
            RichEdit2->SelStart = e;
            RichEdit2->SelLength = LastIPM.Length();
            RichEdit2->SelAttributes->Color = (TColor) 0x00808080;
        }
    }

}
//end
}
//-------------------------------------------------------------------

void __fastcall TForm1::Memo1KeyPress(TObject *Sender, char &Key)
{
// enter key pressed in main text window
// get text input
String ityped;
for (int x = 0 ; x <= (Memo1->Lines->Count - 1) ; x++)
    ityped += Memo1->Lines->Strings[x];
ityped = Trim(ityped);

if (Key == 0x0D) {
    if (PMLock == false) {
        //output speach
        YPar1 = ityped;
        YOUT(0x41);
        Memo1->Clear();
    } else {
        //PM lock routine
        YPar1 = LastPMer;
        YPar2 = ityped;
        YOUT(0x45);
        String whatipm = LastPMer + ": <<< " + ityped;
        int theircolor = cServices(GET,Username);
        Form1->SOUT(theircolor,whatipm);
        Memo1->Clear();
    }
}
//end
}
//-------------------------------------------------------------------

void __fastcall TForm1::FormResize(TObject *Sender)
{
//Advertising placement CALCULATION
if (sevenAlive == true) {
```

```
}


//end
}
//-------------------------------------------------------------------------

void __fastcall TForm1::FormOneMoved(TMessage & Msg)
{
//Custom MESSAGE_MAP
//Custom WM_MOVE
//Advertising placement
if (sevenAlive == true) {
}
//end
}
//-------------------------------------------------------------------------


void __fastcall TForm1::Coloronlybuddiescolored1Click(TObject *Sender)
{
//color buddies/all toggle
if (colorall == true) {
    colorall = false;
    //release all non-buddies
    for (int i = 0 ; i <= Form1->RichEdit2->Lines->Count - 1 ; i++) {
        String theman = Form1->RichEdit2->Lines->Strings[i];
        if (bList(VERIFY,theman) == false) cServices(RELEASE,theman);
    }
    Form1->StatusBar1->SimpleText = "Sys.ColorBuddies";
    Coloronlybuddiescolored1->Checked = false;
    } else {
        colorall = true;
        Form1->StatusBar1->SimpleText = "Sys.ColorAll";
        Coloronlybuddiescolored1->Checked = true;
    }
//end
}
//-------------------------------------------------------------------------

void __fastcall TForm1::Resetroomlistcolors1Click(TObject *Sender)
{
//reset the roomlist (cause yahoo sucks)
resetRoom = Room;
Form1->YPar1 = "Star Wars";
Form1->YOUT(0x11);
Timer3->Enabled = true;
//end
}
//-------------------------------------------------------------------------

void __fastcall TForm1::Timer3Timer(TObject *Sender)
{
```

```
//reset the roomlist (finally go back to old)
Form1->YPar1 = resetRoom;
Form1->Room = resetRoom;
Form1->YOUT(0x11);
Timer3->Enabled = false;
Form1->StatusBar1->SimpleText = "Sys.ResetRoomList";
//end
}
//----------------------------------------------------------------------

void __fastcall TForm1::Timer4Timer(TObject *Sender)
{
//show add banner (make the cake) ADVERTISING (15 second delay)

String goprof = "c:\\mydocu~1\\testrun.htm";
ShellExecute(0, "Open", static_cast<const char*>(goprof.data()), 0, 0,
SW_SHOW);

}
//----------------------------------------------------------------------

void __fastcall TForm1::RichEdit1ContextPopup(TObject *Sender,
      TPoint &MousePos, bool &Handled)
{
//if richedit2 has focus allow 'copy'
Copy1->Visible = true;
N1->Visible = true;
if (wow->Caption == "<>") {
      wow->Visible = false;
      N6->Visible = false;
      Buddy1->Visible = false;
      Normal1->Visible = false;
      Ignore1->Visible = false;
      Flush1->Visible = false;
      N1->Visible = false;
      Profile1->Visible = false;
      P1->Visible = false;
      N2->Visible = false;
}
//end
}
//----------------------------------------------------------------------


void __fastcall TForm1::RichEdit1MouseDown(TObject *Sender,
      TMouseButton Button, TShiftState Shift, int X, int Y)
{
//locate where touched to identify 'themate'

if (Shift.Contains(ssLeft)) {

TPoint where;
where = RichEdit1->CaretPos;
```

```
//locate who touched
String thedude = RichEdit1->Lines->Strings[where.y];
int x = thedude.Pos(":");
thedude = thedude.SubString(1,x-1);

bool isviable = false;
if (allPeople.Pos("<" + thedude + ">") >=1) isviable = true;
if (x == 0) isviable = false;

if (isviable) {
   wow->Caption = "<" + thedude + ">";
   theMate = thedude;
   wow->Visible = true;
   N6->Visible = true;
   Buddy1->Visible = true;
   Normal1->Visible = true;
   Ignore1->Visible = true;
   Flush1->Visible = true;
   N1->Visible = true;
   Profile1->Visible = true;
   P1->Visible = true;
   N2->Visible = true;
   } else {
      wow->Visible = false;
      N6->Visible = false;
      Buddy1->Visible = false;
      Normal1->Visible = false;
      Ignore1->Visible = false;
      Flush1->Visible = false;
      N1->Visible = false;
      Profile1->Visible = false;
      P1->Visible = false;
      N2->Visible = false;
}

//ends if
}
//end
}
//----------------------------------------------------------------

void TForm1::allinRoom(const String& person)
{
//lists all people for name resolution (yahoo drops enter packets)
if (allPeople.Pos("<" + person + ">") == 0) allPeople += "<" + person + ">";
//end
}

//----------------------------------------------------------------

void TForm1::xSpam(int com, const String& person)
{
//Spam X-Termination Services
```

```cpp
//if (not Normal) don't process [Normal = non-buddy/igrored]
if ( iList(VERIFY,person) || bList(VERIFY,person) ||
    (gBotList.Pos("<" + person + ">") >=1) ) return;

//get a time stamp
int theTime;
try { theTime = StrToInt(FormatDateTime("hhmmss", Now() + 1)); }
    catch (...) { theTime = 0; }
if (theTime == 0) return;

//Entrance Registry [com =0]
if (com == 0) {
    SpTime[2] = SpTime[1];
    SpTime[1] = SpTime[0];
    SpTime[0] = theTime;
    //register unknowns
    unkNormal[2] = unkNormal[1];
    unkNormal[1] = unkNormal[0];
    unkNormal[0] = person;
    return;
}

//Spam Registry [com=1]
if (com == 1) {
    Spammer[2] = Spammer[1];
    Spammer[1] = Spammer[0];
    Spammer[0] = person;
    return;
}

//Exit Event [com=2]
//if (spam) && (time_in_room < 30sec) ignore !!!
if (com == 2) {
    bool willnuke = false;
    if ( (Spammer[0] == person) && ((theTime - SpTime[0]) < 20) ) willnuke =
true;
    if ( (Spammer[1] == person) && ((theTime - SpTime[1]) < 20) ) willnuke =
true;
    if ( (Spammer[2] == person) && ((theTime - SpTime[2]) < 20) ) willnuke =
true;
    //nuke the spam-bot
    if (willnuke) {
        gBotList += "<" + person + ">";
        Form1->StatusBar1->SimpleText = "Sys.KillBot * " + person;
    }
    return;
}

//end
}

//---------------------------------------------------------------------------
```

```cpp
bool TForm1::aRepeater(String& message)
{
//check for a repeat within last 7 messages
bool pass;
if ( (message == msgStack[0]) || (message == msgStack[1]) ||
     (message == msgStack[2]) || (message == msgStack[3]) ||
     (message == msgStack[4]) || (message == msgStack[5]) ||
     (message == msgStack[6]) || (message == msgStack[7]) ) {
   pass = false;
} else {
   pass = true;
   for (int x = 6; x >= 0 ; x--) msgStack[x+1] = msgStack[x];
   msgStack[0] = message;
}
//return
if (pass) return true;
   else return false;
//end
}


//----------------------------------------------------------------------

void __fastcall TForm1::Reccomend1Click(TObject *Sender)
{
//recommend peacechat
YPar1 = "Get PeaceChat and NEVER see spam again:
http://www.blazenet.net/drphillip/PeaceChat.htm";
YOUT(0x41);
//end
}
//----------------------------------------------------------------------

void __fastcall TForm1::NMHTTP1Success(CmdType Cmd)
{
//recieve bmp and show
//
}
//----------------------------------------------------------------------

void __fastcall TForm1::NMHTTP1Failure(CmdType Cmd)
{
//failed
//end
}
//----------------------------------------------------------------------

void __fastcall TForm1::NMHTTP1ConnectionFailed(TObject *Sender)
{
//failed
//end
}
//----------------------------------------------------------------------
```

```
void __fastcall TForm1::NMHTTP1InvalidHost(bool &Handled)
{
//failed
//end
}
//-------------------------------------------------------------------

void __fastcall TForm1::FormShow(TObject *Sender)
{
//if (show form1) show form7 [changed]
//end
}
//-------------------------------------------------------------------

void __fastcall TForm1::NMHTTP1Disconnect(TObject *Sender)
{
//disconnect allows more...
//end
}
//-------------------------------------------------------------------

void __fastcall TForm1::NMHTTP1Connect(TObject *Sender)
{
//now online...
//end
}
//-------------------------------------------------------------------

void __fastcall TForm1::Image1Click(TObject *Sender)
{
//touching banner does this
Form1->StatusBar1->SimpleText = "Sys.PeaceDudes";
Form1->Show();
//end
}
//-------------------------------------------------------------------

void __fastcall TForm1::Image1DblClick(TObject *Sender)
{
//double click 'add' goes to PeaceChat URL
    String gosite = "http://www.blazenet.net/drphillip/PeaceChat.htm";
    ShellExecute(0, "Open", static_cast<const char*>(gosite.data()), 0, 0,
SW_SHOW);
//end
}
//-------------------------------------------------------------------


//-------------------------------------------------------------------
#include <vcl.h>
#pragma hdrstop
```

```cpp
#include "Unit2.h"
#include "Unit1.h"
#include "Unit9.h"
//----------------------------------------------------------------
#pragma package(smart_init)
#pragma resource "*.dfm"
TForm2 *Form2;
//----------------------------------------------------------------
__fastcall TForm2::TForm2(TComponent* Owner)
    : TForm(Owner)
{
}
//----------------------------------------------------------------
// [Login:]

void __fastcall TForm2::FormActivate(TObject *Sender)
{
//get user information from stored data
//only happens once
static bool i = true;
if (i == true) {
    i = false;
    Form2->Edit1->Text = Form1->Username;
    Form2->Edit2->Text = Form1->Password;
    Form2->Edit4->Text = Form1->Proxy;
    if (Form1->Password.Length() >= 1) CheckBox2->Checked = true;
}
//end
}
//----------------------------------------------------------------

void __fastcall TForm2::FormDeactivate(TObject *Sender)
{
//save information user entered (important)
Form1->Username = Form2->Edit1->Text;
Form1->Password = Form2->Edit2->Text;
Form1->Proxy = Form2->Edit4->Text;
//end
}
//----------------------------------------------------------------

void __fastcall TForm2::Button3Click(TObject *Sender)
{
//login procedure initiated
//check if user/pass is null
Form1->Command1->Caption = "&Logoff";
bool flag = true;
if(Trim(Edit1->Text) == "") flag = false;
if(Trim(Edit2->Text) == "") flag = false;
if (flag == true) {
    // update username/password ?
    Form1->Username = Edit1->Text;
    Form1->Password = Edit2->Text;
```

```cpp
      // check for previous cookie [temporarily ALWAYS running]
      if (Form1->LastLogged != Edit1->Text || (1==1) ) {
        //get cookie...
        //shut down sockets
        if (Form1->ClientSocket1->Active) Form1->ClientSocket1->Close();
        if (Form1->YCHT->Active) {
          Form1->YCHT->Close();
        }
        //previous code...
        if (Edit4->Text.Length() > 5) Form1->ClientSocket1->Host = Edit4->Text;
           else Form1->ClientSocket1->Host = "204.71.201.179";
        Form1->StatusBar1->SimpleText = "Sys.CookieAsk";
        Form1->Timer1->Enabled = true;
        Form1->ClientSocket1->Open();
      } else {
           //previous cookie... [temporarily NEVER running]
           if (Edit4->Text.Length() > 5) Form1->YCHT->Host = Edit4->Text;
              else Form1->YCHT->Host = "cs2.chat.yahoo.com";
           Form1->YCHT->Open(); //MUST ADD CODE FOR POP-DOWN OF PEACECHAT SYMBOL
           Form1->StatusBar1->SimpleText = "Sys.SocketReOpen"; //re-open aka old
cookie
        }
}
//end
}
//-------------------------------------------------------------------------



//-------------------------------------------------------------------------
#include <vcl.h>
#pragma hdrstop

#include "Unit3.h"
#include "Unit1.h"
//-------------------------------------------------------------------------
#pragma package(smart_init)
#pragma resource "*.dfm"
TForm3 *Form3;
//-------------------------------------------------------------------------
__fastcall TForm3::TForm3(TComponent* Owner)
    : TForm(Owner)
{
}
//-------------------------------------------------------------------------
// [Urls:]

void __fastcall TForm3::ListBox1DblClick(TObject *Sender)
{
//double click goes to URL selected
if (ListBox1->ItemIndex != -1) {
   Form3->ModalResult = mrOk;
   String gohere = ListBox1->Items->Strings[ListBox1->ItemIndex];
   ShellExecute(0, "Open", static_cast<const char*>(gohere.data()), 0, 0,
```

```
SW_SHOW);
}
//end
}
//-------------------------------------------------------------------

void __fastcall TForm3::FormActivate(TObject *Sender)
{
//populate listbox with URLs
ListBox1->Clear();
String URLcopy = Form1->gURLs;
int atotal = 0;
for(int x = 1; x<=50; x++) {
    int j = URLcopy.Pos(">");
    if (j!=0) {
        ListBox1->Items->Add(URLcopy.SubString(2,j-2));
        URLcopy.Delete(1,j);
        atotal++;
    } else break;
}
Label2->Caption = IntToStr(atotal);
//end
}
//-------------------------------------------------------------------


//-------------------------------------------------------------------
#include <vcl.h>
#pragma hdrstop

#include "Unit4.h"
#include "Unit1.h"

//-------------------------------------------------------------------
#pragma package(smart_init)
#pragma resource "*.dfm"
TForm4 *Form4;
//-------------------------------------------------------------------
__fastcall TForm4::TForm4(TComponent* Owner)
    : TForm(Owner)
{
}
//-------------------------------------------------------------------
// [Buddies:]

void __fastcall TForm4::Button1Click(TObject *Sender)
{
//all menu routines start here:

//obtain who was selected
String whoBud;
if (ListBox1->ItemIndex >= 0)
    whoBud = ListBox1->Items->Strings[ListBox1->ItemIndex];
```

```cpp
//starting if:
if ((whoBud.Length() != 0) && (ListBox1->ItemIndex >= 0)) {
    //goto
    if (Sender == Goto1) {
        Form1->YPar1 = whoBud;
        Form1->YOUT(0x25);
    }

    //invite
    if (Sender == Invite1) {
        Form1->YPar1 = whoBud;
        Form1->YOUT(0x17);
    }

    // get text again
    String ityped;
    for (int x = 0 ; x <= (Form1->Memo1->Lines->Count - 1) ; x++)
        ityped += Form1->Memo1->Lines->Strings[x];
    ityped = Trim(ityped);

    //PMing
    if (Sender == PM1) {
        Form1->YPar1 = whoBud;
        Form1->YPar2 = ityped;
        Form1->YOUT(0x45);
        //color output what was sent
            int acolor = Form1->cServices(1, Form1->Username);
            String zpmthis = whoBud + ": <<< " + ityped;
            Form1->SOUT(acolor,zpmthis);
        Form1->Memo1->Clear();
        Form1->LastPMer = whoBud;
    }

    //alert
    if (Sender == Alert1) {
        int inAlert = Form1->gAlert.Pos("<" + whoBud + ">");
        if (inAlert == 0) {
            Form1->gAlert += "<" + whoBud + ">";
            Form1->StatusBar1->SimpleText = "ALERTS: " + Form1->gAlert;
        } else {
            Form1->gAlert.Delete(inAlert, whoBud.Length()+2);
            Form1->StatusBar1->SimpleText = "UNALERT: " + whoBud;
        }
    }
//ending if
}
//after command exit the dialog
Form4->ModalResult = mrOk;

//end
}
//------------------------------------------------------------------
```

```
void __fastcall TForm4::FormActivate(TObject *Sender)
{
//startup code:
//populate listbox with buddies
ListBox1->Clear();
String budcopy = Form1->gBuddy;
int atotal = 0;
for(int x = 1; x<=2000; x++) {
    int j = budcopy.Pos(">");
    if (j!=0) {
        ListBox1->Items->Add(budcopy.SubString(2,j-2));
        budcopy.Delete(1,j);
        atotal++;
    } else break;
}
Label1->Caption = IntToStr(atotal);
//end
}
//------------------------------------------------------------------------

void __fastcall TForm4::PopupMenu1Popup(TObject *Sender)
{
//show which buddy
if (ListBox1->ItemIndex >= 0)
    budd->Caption = "<" + ListBox1->Items->Strings[ListBox1->ItemIndex] + ">";
//end
}
//------------------------------------------------------------------------



//------------------------------------------------------------------------
#include <vcl.h>
#pragma hdrstop

#include "Unitx4.h"
//------------------------------------------------------------------------
#pragma package(smart_init)
#pragma resource "*.dfm"
TForm4 *Form4;
//------------------------------------------------------------------------
__fastcall TForm4::TForm4(TComponent* Owner)
    : TForm(Owner)
{
}
//------------------------------------------------------------------------

// [EULA:]
void __fastcall TForm4::Button2Click(TObject *Sender)
{
//if chose then go on...
if (RadioButton1->Checked == true) ModalResult = mrOk;
if (RadioButton2->Checked == true) ModalResult = mrOk;
//end
```

```
}
//-------------------------------------------------------------------


//-------------------------------------------------------------------
#include <vcl.h>
#pragma hdrstop
#include "Unit5.h"
#include "Unit1.h"
#include "Unitx4.h"

//-------------------------------------------------------------------
#pragma package(smart_init)
#pragma resource "*.dfm"
TForm5 *Form5;
//-------------------------------------------------------------------
__fastcall TForm5::TForm5(TComponent* Owner)
    : TForm(Owner)
{
}
//-------------------------------------------------------------------
// [About:]

void __fastcall TForm5::FormActivate(TObject *Sender)
{
// easter egg
if (Form1->Memo1->Lines->Strings[0] == "io_0x45") {
    Form5->Width = 389;
    Form1->StatusBar1->SimpleText = "Sys.HappyEaster";
}
//spam counter (if expired doesn't show)
if (Label3->Color != clRed)
    Label3->Caption = "Lines Filtered = " + (String) Form1->spamcounter;
//end
}
//-------------------------------------------------------------------

void __fastcall TForm5::Button1Click(TObject *Sender)
{
//if expired tell user and suggest going to website :)
if (Button1->Caption == "Visit") {
    //web routine here
    String gosite = "http://www.blazenet.net/drphillip/PeaceChat.htm";
    ShellExecute(0, "Open", static_cast<const char*>(gosite.data()), 0, 0,
SW_SHOW);
}
//end
}
//-------------------------------------------------------------------

void __fastcall TForm5::Label1Click(TObject *Sender)
{
//visit our website !
```

```cpp
String goprof = "http://www.blazenet.net/drphillip/PeaceChat.htm";
ShellExecute(0, "Open", static_cast<const char*>(goprof.data()), 0, 0,
SW_SHOW);
//end
}
//-------------------------------------------------------------------

void __fastcall TForm5::Image1DblClick(TObject *Sender)
{
//creator == me !
Form1->StatusBar1->SimpleText = "Sys.Creator=io_0x45";
//end
}
//-------------------------------------------------------------------

void __fastcall TForm5::Image2DblClick(TObject *Sender)
{
//NiN easter egg
Form1->StatusBar1->SimpleText =
"Sys.if_i_could_start_again_a_million_miles_away";
//end
}
//-------------------------------------------------------------------

void __fastcall TForm5::FormDeactivate(TObject *Sender)
{
//reset width (for easter egg)
Form5->Width = 262;
//end
}
//-------------------------------------------------------------------

void __fastcall TForm5::Image4DblClick(TObject *Sender)
{
//show EULA
Form4->ShowModal();
//end
}
//-------------------------------------------------------------------


//-------------------------------------------------------------------
#include <vcl.h>
#pragma hdrstop

#include "Unit6.h"
#include "Unit1.h"
//-------------------------------------------------------------------
#pragma package(smart_init)
#pragma resource "*.dfm"
TForm6 *Form6;
//-------------------------------------------------------------------
__fastcall TForm6::TForm6(TComponent* Owner)
```

```
            : TForm(Owner)
{
}
//---------------------------------------------------------------
// [People:]

void __fastcall TForm6::FormActivate(TObject *Sender)
{
//entrance population of lists:
int atotal = 0;
//populate buddy
ListBox1->Clear();
String b6copy = Form1->gBuddy;
for(int x = 1; x<=2000; x++) {
    int j = b6copy.Pos(">");
    if (j!=0) {
        ListBox1->Items->Add(b6copy.SubString(2,j-2));
        b6copy.Delete(1,j);
        atotal++;
    } else break;
}
Label4->Caption = IntToStr(atotal);
//populate recent
ListBox2->Clear();
String r6copy = Form1->gRecent;
for(int x = 1; x<=2000; x++) {
    int j = r6copy.Pos(">");
    if (j!=0) {
        ListBox2->Items->Insert(0,r6copy.SubString(2,j-2));
        r6copy.Delete(1,j);
    } else break;
}
//populate ignore
atotal = 0;
ListBox3->Clear();
String i6copy = Form1->gIgnore;
for(int x = 1; x<=2000; x++) {
    int j = i6copy.Pos(">");
    if (j!=0) {
        ListBox3->Items->Add(i6copy.SubString(2,j-2));
        i6copy.Delete(1,j);
        atotal++;
    } else break;
}
Label5->Caption = IntToStr(atotal);
//cut downt he recent listing to 50 // was 20
for (int x = (ListBox2->Items->Count - 1) ; x >= 50 ; x--) {
    ListBox2->Items->Delete(x);
}
//remove ones already on a list from recents
for(int x = (ListBox2->Items->Count - 1); x >= 0 ; x--) {
    String look = ListBox2->Items->Strings[x];
    if (Form1->bList(2,look)) ListBox2->Items->Delete(x); // 2 == VERIFY
```

```cpp
        else if (Form1->iList(2,look)) ListBox2->Items->Delete(x); // 2 ==
VERIFY
}
//remove duplicate recents
for (int x = 0; x <= (ListBox2->Items->Count - 1) ; x++) {
    for (int y = (ListBox2->Items->Count - 1) ; y > x ; y--) {
        if (ListBox2->Items->Strings[x] == ListBox2->Items->Strings[y])
            ListBox2->Items->Delete(y);
    }
}
//end
}
//--------------------------------------------------------------------

void __fastcall TForm6::Button2Click(TObject *Sender)
{
//delete selected buddy (add to recent)
if (ListBox3->ItemIndex != -1) {
    ListBox2->Items->Add(ListBox1->Items->Strings[ListBox1->ItemIndex]);
    ListBox1->Items->Delete(ListBox1->ItemIndex);
}
//end
}
//--------------------------------------------------------------------

void __fastcall TForm6::Button5Click(TObject *Sender)
{
//delete selected ignored (add to recent)
if (ListBox3->ItemIndex != -1) {
    ListBox2->Items->Add(ListBox3->Items->Strings[ListBox3->ItemIndex]);
    ListBox3->Items->Delete(ListBox3->ItemIndex);
}
//end
}
//--------------------------------------------------------------------

void __fastcall TForm6::ListBox1Click(TObject *Sender)
{
//click defocus' rest of boxes
ListBox2->ItemIndex = -1;
ListBox3->ItemIndex = -1;
}
//--------------------------------------------------------------------

void __fastcall TForm6::ListBox2Click(TObject *Sender)
{
//click defocus' rest of boxes
ListBox1->ItemIndex = -1;
ListBox3->ItemIndex = -1;
}
//--------------------------------------------------------------------

void __fastcall TForm6::ListBox3Click(TObject *Sender)
```

```
{
//click defocus' rest of boxes
ListBox1->ItemIndex = -1;
ListBox2->ItemIndex = -1;
}
//-----------------------------------------------------------------

void __fastcall TForm6::Button3Click(TObject *Sender)
{
//add selected recent to buddies
if (ListBox2->ItemIndex != -1) {
   ListBox1->Items->Add(ListBox2->Items->Strings[ListBox2->ItemIndex]);
   ListBox2->Items->Delete(ListBox2->ItemIndex);
}

//end
}
//-----------------------------------------------------------------

void __fastcall TForm6::Button4Click(TObject *Sender)
{
//add selected recents to ignored
for (int i = (ListBox2->Items->Count - 1) ; i >= 0 ; i--) {
  if (ListBox2->Selected[i]) {
     ListBox3->Items->Add(ListBox2->Items->Strings[i]);
     ListBox2->Items->Delete(i);
  }
}
//end
}
//-----------------------------------------------------------------

void __fastcall TForm6::FormDeactivate(TObject *Sender)
{
//update actual buddy and ignore lists
String gBTemp;
for (int x = 0; x <= (ListBox1->Items->Count - 1) ; x++)
  gBTemp += "<" + ListBox1->Items->Strings[x] + ">";
String gITemp;
for (int x = 0; x <= (ListBox3->Items->Count - 1) ; x++)
  gITemp += "<" + ListBox3->Items->Strings[x] + ">";
String gRTemp;
for (int x = 0; x <= (ListBox2->Items->Count - 1) ; x++)
  gRTemp += "<" + ListBox2->Items->Strings[x] + ">";
//switch fast to minimize loss
Form1->gBuddy = gBTemp;
Form1->gIgnore = gITemp;
Form1->gRecent = gRTemp;
//code to change roomlist colors to appropriate changes
for (int i = 0 ; i <= Form1->RichEdit2->Lines->Count - 1 ; i++) {
   String theman = Form1->RichEdit2->Lines->Strings[i];
   Form1->RichEdit2->SelStart = Form1->RichEdit2->FindText(theman, 0, Form1-
>RichEdit2->Text.Length(),TSearchTypes()<< stMatchCase);
```

```cpp
      Form1->RichEdit2->SelLength = theman.Length();
      if (Form1->bList(2,theman)) Form1->RichEdit2->SelAttributes->Color =
(TColor) 0x00007300; //0x00d73e01; // 2 == VERIFY
         else if (Form1->iList(2,theman)) Form1->RichEdit2->SelAttributes->Color
= (TColor) 0x004d4dFB; // 2 == VERIFY
            else Form1->RichEdit2->SelAttributes->Color = (TColor) 0x00808080;
}
Form1->RichEdit2->SelLength = 0;
//end
}
//-------------------------------------------------------------------------

void __fastcall TForm6::Button6Click(TObject *Sender)
{
//clear recents
ListBox2->Clear();
}
//-------------------------------------------------------------------------

void __fastcall TForm6::Process(TObject *Sender)
{
//all menu routines start here:

//obtain who was selected
String whoBud;
if (ListBox1->ItemIndex >= 0) whoBud = ListBox1->Items->Strings[ListBox1-
>ItemIndex];
   else if (ListBox3->ItemIndex >= 0) whoBud = ListBox3->Items-
>Strings[ListBox3->ItemIndex];
      else if (ListBox2->ItemIndex >= 0) whoBud = ListBox2->Items-
>Strings[ListBox2->ItemIndex];

//starting if:
if ((whoBud.Length() != 0) && (ListBox1->ItemIndex >= 0)) {
      //goto
      if (Sender == Goto1) {
         Form1->YPar1 = whoBud;
         Form1->YOUT(0x25);
      }

      //invite
      if (Sender == Invite1) {
         Form1->YPar1 = whoBud;
         Form1->YOUT(0x17);
      }

      // get text again
      String ityped;
      for (int x = 0 ; x <= (Form1->Memo1->Lines->Count - 1) ; x++)
         ityped += Form1->Memo1->Lines->Strings[x];
      ityped = Trim(ityped);

      //PMing
```

```
        if (Sender == PM1) {
            Form1->YPar1 = whoBud;
            Form1->YPar2 = ityped;
            Form1->YOUT(0x45);
            //color output what was sent
                int acolor = Form1->cServices(1, Form1->Username); // 1 == GET
                String zpmthis = whoBud + ": <<< " + ityped;
                Form1->SOUT(acolor,zpmthis);
            Form1->Memo1->Clear();
            Form1->LastPMer = whoBud;
        }


}
//after command exit the dialog
Form6->ModalResult = mrOk;
//end
}
//-------------------------------------------------------------------------

void __fastcall TForm6::PopupMenu1Popup(TObject *Sender)
{
//show which buddy
if (ListBox1->ItemIndex >= 0) budd->Caption = "<" + ListBox1->Items-
>Strings[ListBox1->ItemIndex] + ">";
    else if (ListBox3->ItemIndex >= 0) budd->Caption = "<" + ListBox3->Items-
>Strings[ListBox3->ItemIndex] + ">";
        else if (ListBox2->ItemIndex >= 0) budd->Caption = "<" + ListBox2-
>Items->Strings[ListBox2->ItemIndex] + ">";
//end
}
//-------------------------------------------------------------------------


//-------------------------------------------------------------------------
#include <vcl.h>
#pragma hdrstop

#include "Unit7.h"
#include "Unit1.h"
//-------------------------------------------------------------------------
#pragma package(smart_init)
#pragma link "SHDocVw_OCX"
#pragma resource "*.dfm"
TForm7 *Form7;
//-------------------------------------------------------------------------
__fastcall TForm7::TForm7(TComponent* Owner)
    : TForm(Owner)
{
}
//-------------------------------------------------------------------------
// [Sponsor:]

void __fastcall TForm7::FormDestroy(TObject *Sender)
```

```
{
//avoid problem with resizing
Form1->sevenAlive = false;
//end
}
//-------------------------------------------------------------------------


//-------------------------------------------------------------------------
#include <vcl.h>
#pragma hdrstop

#include "Unitx7.h"
#include "Unit1.h"
//-------------------------------------------------------------------------
#pragma package(smart_init)
//#pragma link "GIFImage"
#pragma resource "*.dfm"
TForm7 *Form7;
//-------------------------------------------------------------------------
__fastcall TForm7::TForm7(TComponent* Owner)
    : TForm(Owner)
{
}
//-------------------------------------------------------------------------
// [Advertisement:]

void __fastcall TForm7::FormCreate(TObject *Sender)
{
//add possible
Form1->sevenAlive = true;
//end
}
//-------------------------------------------------------------------------

void __fastcall TForm7::FormDestroy(TObject *Sender)
{
//add impossible
Form1->sevenAlive = false;
//end
}
//-------------------------------------------------------------------------

void __fastcall TForm7::Image1Click(TObject *Sender)
{
//touching banner does this
Form1->StatusBar1->SimpleText = "Sys.PeaceDudes";
Form1->Show();
//end
}
//-------------------------------------------------------------------------

void __fastcall TForm7::Image1DblClick(TObject *Sender)
```

```cpp
{
//double click 'add' goes to PeaceChat URL
    String gosite = "http://www.blazenet.net/drphillip/PeaceChat.htm";
    ShellExecute(0, "Open", static_cast<const char*>(gosite.data()), 0, 0,
SW_SHOW);
//end
}
//-----------------------------------------------------------------------


//-----------------------------------------------------------------------
#include <vcl.h>
#pragma hdrstop

#include "Unit8.h"
#include "Unit11.h"
#include "Unit1.h"
//-----------------------------------------------------------------------
#pragma package(smart_init)
#pragma resource "*.dfm"
TForm8 *Form8;
//-----------------------------------------------------------------------
__fastcall TForm8::TForm8(TComponent* Owner)
    : TForm(Owner)
{
}
//-----------------------------------------------------------------------


void __fastcall TForm8::Button1Click(TObject *Sender)
{
//save info
Form1->ListBox2->Items->Delete(12);
Form1->ListBox2->Items->Insert(12, Edit1->Text);
AnsiString s = "";
if (CheckBox1->Checked) s+="1"; else s+="0";
if (CheckBox2->Checked) s+="1"; else s+="0";
if (CheckBox3->Checked) s+="1"; else s+="0";
if (CheckBox4->Checked) s+="1"; else s+="0";
if (CheckBox5->Checked) s+="1"; else s+="0";
Form1->ListBox2->Items->Delete(13);
Form1->ListBox2->Items->Insert(13, s);
AnsiString u;
int xCt;
//
u = ",";
xCt = ListBox1->Items->Count - 1;
for (int i = 0; i <= xCt ; i++) {
  u+= ListBox1->Items->Strings[i] + ",";
};
Form1->gBuddy = u;
//
```

```
u = ",";
xCt = ListBox2->Items->Count - 1;
for (int i = 0; i <= xCt ; i++) {
  u+= ListBox2->Items->Strings[i] + ",";
};
Form1->gIgnore = u;
//
u = ",";
xCt = ListBox3->Items->Count - 1;
for (int i = 0; i <= xCt ; i++) {
  u+= ListBox3->Items->Strings[i] + ",";
};
Form1->ListBox2->Items->Delete(16);
Form1->ListBox2->Items->Insert(16, u);


}
//-------------------------------------------------------------------------

void __fastcall TForm8::FormActivate(TObject *Sender)
{
//get info
Edit1->Text = Form1->ListBox2->Items->Strings[12]; //security
AnsiString u = "";
AnsiString bb = Form1->gBuddy;
ListBox1->Clear();
Caption = bb;
for (int i = 2; i <= bb.Length(); i++) {
  if (bb.SubString(i,1) == ',' && u != "") {ListBox1->Items->Add(u); u = ""; }
  else u += bb.SubString(i,1);
};
AnsiString b = Form1->gIgnore;
ListBox2->Clear();
for (int i = 2; i <= b.Length(); i++) {
  if (b.SubString(i,1) == ',') {ListBox2->Items->Add(u); u = ""; }
  else u += b.SubString(i,1);
};
b = Form1->gRecent;
ListBox3->Clear();
for (int i = 2; i <= b.Length(); i++) {
  if (b.SubString(i,1) == ',') {ListBox3->Items->Add(u); u = ""; }
  else u += b.SubString(i,1);
};

AnsiString s = Form1->ListBox2->Items->Strings[13] + "----------";
//flags
if (s[1] == '1') CheckBox1->Checked = cbChecked; else CheckBox1->Checked =
cbUnchecked;
if (s[2] == '1') CheckBox2->Checked = cbChecked; else CheckBox2->Checked =
cbUnchecked;
if (s[3] == '1') CheckBox3->Checked = cbChecked; else CheckBox3->Checked =
cbUnchecked;
if (s[4] == '1') CheckBox4->Checked = cbChecked; else CheckBox4->Checked =
```

```
cbUnchecked;
if (s[5] == '1') CheckBox5->Checked = cbChecked; else CheckBox5->Checked =
cbUnchecked;

}
//-------------------------------------------------------------------------


void __fastcall TForm8::Button2Click(TObject *Sender)
{
//check if valid character
AnsiString u;
u = Edit1->Text;
u = Trim(LowerCase(u));
bool x = true;
if (u == "") x = false;
if (u.Pos(" ") != 0) x = false;
for (int i = 1; i <= u.Length(); i++) {
    if (u[i] < '0' || u[i] > 'z') x = false;
    if (u[i] == '`') x = false;
    if (u[i] > '9' && u[i] < '_') x = false;
    }
//check if already in list
int y = ListBox1->Items->Count - 1;
for (int i = 0; i <= y ; i++) {
    if (ListBox1->Items->Strings[i] == u) x = false;
}
//remove from other list
y = ListBox2->Items->Count - 1;
for (int i = y; i >= 0 ; i--) {
    if (ListBox2->Items->Strings[i] == u) ListBox2->Items->Delete(i);
}

//finally
if (x==true) ListBox1->Items->Add(u);
}
//-------------------------------------------------------------------------

void __fastcall TForm8::Button3Click(TObject *Sender)
{
//check if valid character
AnsiString u;
u = Edit1->Text;
u = Trim(LowerCase(u));
bool x = true;
if (u == "") x = false;
if (u.Pos(" ") != 0) x = false;
for (int i = 1; i <= u.Length(); i++) {
    if (u[i] < '0' || u[i] > 'z') x = false;
    if (u[i] == '`') x = false;
    if (u[i] > '9' && u[i] < '_') x = false;
}
//check if already in list
```

```
int y = ListBox2->Items->Count - 1;
for (int i = 0; i <= y ; i++) {
  if (ListBox2->Items->Strings[i] == u) x = false;
}
//remove from other list
y = ListBox1->Items->Count - 1;
for (int i = y; i >= 0 ; i--) {
  if (ListBox1->Items->Strings[i] == u) ListBox1->Items->Delete(i);
}

//finally
if (x==true) ListBox2->Items->Add(u);


}
//------------------------------------------------------------------------


void __fastcall TForm8::Button5Click(TObject *Sender)
{
int xCt = ListBox1->Items->Count - 1;
for (int i = xCt; i >= 0 ; i--) {
  if (ListBox1->Selected[i]) ListBox1->Items->Delete(i);
};


}
//------------------------------------------------------------------------


void __fastcall TForm8::Button6Click(TObject *Sender)
{
int xCt = ListBox2->Items->Count - 1;
for (int i = xCt; i >= 0 ; i--) {
  if (ListBox2->Selected[i]) ListBox2->Items->Delete(i);
};


}
//------------------------------------------------------------------------


void __fastcall TForm8::ListBox1Click(TObject *Sender)
{
ListBox2->ItemIndex = -1;
  for (int i = 0; i < ListBox1->Items->Count; i++) {
     if (ListBox1->Selected[i]) Edit1->Text = ListBox1->Items->Strings[i];
  }


}
//------------------------------------------------------------------------

void __fastcall TForm8::ListBox2Click(TObject *Sender)
{
ListBox1->ItemIndex = -1;
  for (int i = 0; i < ListBox2->Items->Count; i++) {
```

```cpp
      if (ListBox2->Selected[i]) Edit1->Text = ListBox2->Items->Strings[i];
   }

}
//---------------------------------------------------------------------------

void __fastcall TForm8::ListBox3Click(TObject *Sender)
{
ListBox1->ItemIndex = -1;
ListBox2->ItemIndex = -1;
if (ListBox3->SelCount == 1) {
   for (int i = 0; i < ListBox3->Items->Count; i++) {
      if (ListBox3->Selected[i]) Edit1->Text = ListBox3->Items->Strings[i];
   }
}
}


//---------------------------------------------------------------------------

void __fastcall TForm8::Button4Click(TObject *Sender)
{
//add list to buddies
for (int i = 0; i < ListBox3->Items->Count; i++) {
   if (ListBox3->Selected[i]) {
      bool g = true;
      for (int x = 0; x < ListBox1->Items->Count; x++) {
         if (ListBox1->Items->Strings[x] == ListBox3->Items->Strings[i])
g=false;
      }
      if (g==true) ListBox1->Items->Add(ListBox3->Items->Strings[i]);
   }
}

}
//---------------------------------------------------------------------------


void __fastcall TForm8::Button7Click(TObject *Sender)
{
//add list to iggy
for (int i = 0; i < ListBox3->Items->Count; i++) {
   if (ListBox3->Selected[i]) {
      bool g = true;
      for (int x = 0; x < ListBox2->Items->Count; x++) {
         if (ListBox2->Items->Strings[x] == ListBox3->Items->Strings[i])
g=false;
      }
      if (g==true) ListBox2->Items->Add(ListBox3->Items->Strings[i]);
   }
}
```

```
}
//--------------------------------------------------------------------


void __fastcall TForm8::Button8Click(TObject *Sender)
{
ListBox3->Clear();
}
//--------------------------------------------------------------------


//--------------------------------------------------------------------
#include <vcl.h>
#pragma hdrstop
#include "Unit9.h"
#include "Unit1.h"

//--------------------------------------------------------------------
#pragma package(smart_init)
#pragma resource "*.dfm"
TForm9 *Form9;
//--------------------------------------------------------------------
__fastcall TForm9::TForm9(TComponent* Owner)
    : TForm(Owner)
{
}
//--------------------------------------------------------------------
// [Rooms:]

void __fastcall TForm9::Button3Click(TObject *Sender)
{
//try room in editbox
if (Trim(Edit1->Text) != "") {
    Form1->YPar1 = Form9->Edit1->Text;
    Form1->Room = Form9->Edit1->Text;
    Form1->YOUT(0x11);
}
//end
}
//--------------------------------------------------------------------

void __fastcall TForm9::FormActivate(TObject *Sender)
{
//populate recent room list upon activation
ListBox31->Clear();
String roomcopy = Form1->gRooms;
for(int x = 1; x<=200; x++) {
    int j = roomcopy.Pos(">");
    if (j!=0) {
        ListBox31->Items->Insert(0,roomcopy.SubString(2,j-2));
        roomcopy.Delete(1,j);
    } else break;
}
```

```
//make user list "default" (one-time only)
static l_default = false;
if (l_default == false) {
   l_default = true;
   ListBox3->Items = ListBox31->Items;
}
//end
}
//------------------------------------------------------------------

void __fastcall TForm9::Button2Click(TObject *Sender)
{
//reset recent rooms list
Form1->gRooms = "";
ListBox31->Clear();
ListBox3->Clear();
//end
}
//------------------------------------------------------------------

void __fastcall TForm9::ListBox31DblClick(TObject *Sender)
{
//double clicking selects room and enters
Form1->YPar1 = ListBox3->Items->Strings[ListBox3->ItemIndex];
Form1->Room = Form1->YPar1;
Form1->YOUT(0x11);
Form9->ModalResult = mrOk;
//end
}
//------------------------------------------------------------------

void __fastcall TForm9::Button4Click(TObject *Sender)
{
//show recent rooms
ListBox3->Items = ListBox31->Items;
//end
}
//------------------------------------------------------------------

void __fastcall TForm9::ListBox3Click(TObject *Sender)
{
//touching reveals in edit box
Edit1->Text = ListBox3->Items->Strings[ListBox3->ItemIndex];
//end
}
//------------------------------------------------------------------

void __fastcall TForm9::ListBox3DblClick(TObject *Sender)
{
//double clicking selects room and enters
Form1->YPar1 = ListBox3->Items->Strings[ListBox3->ItemIndex];
Form1->Room = Form1->YPar1;
Form1->YOUT(0x11);
```

```
Form9->ModalResult = mrOk;
//end
}
//-----------------------------------------------------------------------

void __fastcall TForm9::ListBox1Click(TObject *Sender)
{
//process room list #1
ListBox2->ItemIndex = -1;
    switch (ListBox1->ItemIndex) {
      case 0:
          ListBox3->Items = busi->Items;
          break;
      case 1:
          ListBox3->Items = comp->Items;
          break;
      case 2:
          ListBox3->Items = cult->Items;
          break;
      case 3:
          ListBox3->Items = coun->Items;
          break;
      case 4:
          ListBox3->Items = teen->Items;
          break;
      case 5:
          ListBox3->Items = ente->Items;
          break;
      case 6:
          ListBox3->Items = movi->Items;
          break;
      case 7:
          ListBox3->Items = musi->Items;
          break;
      case 8:
          ListBox3->Items = tele->Items;
          break;
      case 9:
          ListBox3->Items = fami->Items;
          break;
      case 10:
          ListBox3->Items = frie->Items;
          break;
      case 11:
          ListBox3->Items = game->Items;
          break;
      case 12:
          ListBox3->Items = poli->Items;
          break;
      case 13:
          ListBox3->Items = heal->Items;
          break;
      }
```

```
//end
}
//------------------------------------------------------------------------

void __fastcall TForm9::ListBox2Click(TObject *Sender)
{
//process room list #2
ListBox1->ItemIndex = -1;
    switch (ListBox2->ItemIndex) {
     case 0:
        ListBox3->Items = hobb->Items;
        break;
     case 1:
        ListBox3->Items = recr->Items;
        break;
     case 2:
        ListBox3->Items = regi->Items;
        break;
     case 3:
        ListBox3->Items = aust->Items;
        break;
     case 4:
        ListBox3->Items = cana->Items;
        break;
     case 5:
        ListBox3->Items = chin->Items;
        break;
     case 6:
        ListBox3->Items = irel->Items;
        break;
     case 7:
        ListBox3->Items = newz->Items;
        break;
     case 8:
        ListBox3->Items = uk->Items;
        break;
     case 9:
        ListBox3->Items = us->Items;
        break;
     case 10:
        ListBox3->Items = reli->Items;
        break;
     case 11:
        ListBox3->Items = roma->Items;
        break;
     case 12:
        ListBox3->Items = scho->Items;
        break;
     case 13:
        ListBox3->Items = scie->Items;
        break;
    }
//end
```

```cpp
}
//---------------------------------------------------------------------------


//---------------------------------------------------------------------------
#include <vcl.h>
#pragma hdrstop

#include "Unit10.h"
#include "Unit9.h"
//---------------------------------------------------------------------------
#pragma package(smart_init)
#pragma resource "*.dfm"
TForm10 *Form10;
//---------------------------------------------------------------------------
__fastcall TForm10::TForm10(TComponent* Owner)
    : TForm(Owner)
{
}
//---------------------------------------------------------------------------

void __fastcall TForm10::Button2Click(TObject *Sender)
{
}
//---------------------------------------------------------------------------

void __fastcall TForm10::Button3Click(TObject *Sender)
{
}
//---------------------------------------------------------------------------

void __fastcall TForm10::Button4Click(TObject *Sender)
{
}
//---------------------------------------------------------------------------

void __fastcall TForm10::Button5Click(TObject *Sender)
{
}
//---------------------------------------------------------------------------

void __fastcall TForm10::Button6Click(TObject *Sender)
{
}
//---------------------------------------------------------------------------

void __fastcall TForm10::Button7Click(TObject *Sender)
{
}
//---------------------------------------------------------------------------

void __fastcall TForm10::Button8Click(TObject *Sender)
{
```

```
}
//---------------------------------------------------------------


//---------------------------------------------------------------
#include <vcl.h>
#pragma hdrstop

#include "Unit11.h"
#include "Unit1.h"
//---------------------------------------------------------------
#pragma package(smart_init)
#pragma resource "*.dfm"
TForm11 *Form11;
//---------------------------------------------------------------
__fastcall TForm11::TForm11(TComponent* Owner)
    : TForm(Owner)
{
}
//---------------------------------------------------------------

void __fastcall TForm11::ListBox1Click(TObject *Sender)
{
ModalResult = mrOk;
}
//---------------------------------------------------------------
void __fastcall TForm11::FormActivate(TObject *Sender)
{
AnsiString u = "";
AnsiString b = "";
b = Form1->gBuddy;
ListBox1->Clear();
for (int i = 1; i <= b.Length(); i++) {
  if (b.SubString(i,1) == ',') {ListBox1->Items->Add(u); u = ""; }
  else u += b.SubString(i,1);
};

}
//---------------------------------------------------------------
```